ПЕКИН

BRYN THOMAS was born in Zimbabwe where he grew up on a farm. Since graduating from Durham University with a degree in anthropology, travel on five continents has included a Saharan journey in his home-built kit-car, a solo 2500km cycle ride through the Andes, ten Himalayan treks and 50,000km of rail travel.

The first edition of this book, shortlisted for the Thomas Cook Travel and Guide Book Awards, was the result of several trips on the Trans-Siberian and six months in the Reading Room of the British Library. Subsequent publications have included *Trekking in the Annapurna Region*, also published by Trailblazer, and guides to India, Goa and Britain which he co-authored for Lonely Planet.

In 1991 he set up Trailblazer, to produce the series of route guides for adventurous travellers that has now grown to over 40 titles.

JAMES PITKIN updated the seventh edition of this book. Born in Ohio, James earned a Bachelor's degree in English Literature at Kenyon College before fleeing to Europe. He lived for six years in the Czech Republic, where he worked as a reporter at *The Prague Post* and as a guidebook writer while exploring Central and Eastern Europe. James returned to the United States to work as a reporter in Washington state before updating this book. He currently lives in Portland, Oregon.

Trans-Siberian Handbook
First edition 1988; this seventh edition 2007

Publisher
Trailblazer Publications
The Old Manse, Tower Rd, Hindhead, Surrey, GU26 6SU, UK
Fax (+44) 01428-607571, info@trailblazer-guides.com
www.trailblazer-guides.com

British Library Cataloguing in Publication Data
A catalogue record for this book is available from the British Library

ISBN 978-1-873756-94-2

Cover photograph © Ron Ziel
Other photographs © as credited
Illustrations © Nick Hill

Editor: Clare Weldon
Series editor: Patricia Major
Cartography: Nick Hill
Typesetting: Anna Jacomb-Hood
Layout: Anna Jacomb-Hood, Bryn Thomas, Laura Stone
Proof-reading: Jane Thomas, Laura Stone, Anna Jacomb-Hood
Illustrations: Nick Hill
Cover design: Richard Mayneord
Index: Jane Thomas

Important note
Every effort has been made by the author and publisher to ensure that the information
contained herein is as accurate and up to date as possible. However, they are unable to
accept responsibility for any inconvenience, loss or injury sustained by anyone as a
result of the advice and information given in this guide.

Printed on chlorine-free paper by
D2Print (☎ +65-6295 5598), Singapore

Trans-Siberian
HANDBOOK

B R Y N   T H O M A S

**SEVENTH EDITION RESEARCHED AND UPDATED BY
JAMES PITKIN**

TRAILBLAZER PUBLICATIONS

For our long-suffering Series Editor

Acknowledgements

From James: Many thanks to Bryn Thomas for his help and guidance throughout this project, and as always, to my father, Peter J Pitkin, for his unending support. Thanks also to everyone who assisted me in ways small and large on the road, including Katya Petruchak in St Petersburg; Neil McGowan and his staff at The Russia Experience in Moscow; Michael Mainville in Moscow; Ksenia Urlova in Tobolsk; Grigory Izbenko in Tobolsk; Artyom 'The Jazzman' Urlov in Tyumen; Kirill Vladimirov in Irkutsk; Sergei Yakovlevich on Olkhon Island; Konstantin Bryliakov at Yekaterinburg Guide Center; Slava Tsydenov, Sergei Golubiev and Anastasia Tsydenova in Chita; Fan Yushi in Harbin; Frederick Malouf in Beijing; Bobby and Kim at UB Guesthouse in Ulan Bator; and Syd and Quick Jimmy in Prague.

From Bryn: I am greatly indebted to the numerous people who have helped me with this project since the publication in 1988 of what became, in its second edition, the book that started Trailblazer. I'd particularly like to thank our series editor, Patricia Major, for her unwavering support right from the beginning and for setting the high editorial standards. Thanks also to Jane Thomas not only for the current comprehensive index but also for her extensive work in compiling the original strip maps and town plans. Nick Hill has built on her foundations with consummate skill; I'm grateful to him for the digitized maps, his excellent line drawings and also for all his research work on earlier editions. Thanks also to Clare Weldon for the additional research on Part 1 and for her very thorough editing of the text.

Thanks to James Pitkin for accepting the challenge and researching this seventh edition and also for beefing up the nightlife sections – hope the head's better; Nick Hill, John King and Neil McGowan for updating the sixth edition of the book, Athol Yates for original text on Vladimir, Suzdal and Nizhny Novgorod, the accompanying railway text, the carriage plan and all his and Tatyana Pozar-Burgar's work on the fourth edition of the book; Athol Yates and Nicholas Zvegintzov for the railway dictionary, Dominic Streatfeild-James who updated the third edition (and whose wry comments survive); Doug Streatfeild-James for the Chinese words and phrases section; Neil Taylor (Regent Holidays) for general tips and advice; and Ron Ziel for the cover photograph. Thanks in particular to Richard Mayneord for the fresh new Trailblazer cover design and also for photos; and to Laura Stone for research, proofreading and Cyrillic skills. I am particularly grateful to Anna Jacomb-Hood for researching and updating Part 6, for typesetting and laydown and for so much help in other ways with the production of the book.

Among the readers who wrote: thanks to Alison (NZ), Olga Belnik (Russia), Mahmood Bhutta (UK), James Boyd (Ireland), John Bradford, Simon Calder (UK), Malcolm Carroll (UK), Asger Christiansen (Denmark), Lawrence Cotter (USA), Phil Davies (UK), Lena Davigova (Russia), Christopher Downey (Australia), Laurens den Dulk (Netherlands), Howard Dymock (UK), Col Francis and Christine Emmorey (UK), Jay Gary Finkelstein (USA), Penny Fitt (UK), Julia Fitzgerald, Claudia Gamperle (Switzerland), Emmy Gengler (USA), Yiannis Gikas (Greece), Gordon Gill (USA), Jim Gill (Australia), Jonny Googs (UK), Dmitri Gorokhov (Russia), John Gothard (UK), Tom Grant, Laura Hamelen (UK), Dr Malcolm Hannan (UK), Reijo Härkönen (Finland), Will Harrison-Cripps (UK), Alexander Hartig, Glenn Harvey (Australia), Angela Hollingsworth (UK), Iwan (Russia), Benedikt Jaeger (Germany), Andy Jones (HK), Oskar Karlin, Ruth Kennedy, Dr Mark Krebs, Valeria Kuteeva (Russia), Rowena Lambert, Stu Lloyd (Australia), Matz Lonnedal Risberg (Norway), Karin MacArthur (Australia), Andrea Marcialis (Italy), Laurie Martin (USA), Matheu (UK) & Wieteke (Netherlands), Stephen McLaughlin (UK), Richard Maxey, Terry Nakazono (USA), Yuri Nemirovsky (Russia), Heather Oxley (Egypt), Oded Paporisch (Israel), John Parton, Marcus Patzig (Germany), Rich Perkins (UK), Jakub Pilch (Poland), Helen Revell, Philip Robinson (UK), Nancy Scarth (Canada), Tobi Schwarzmueller (Germany), Rolf Smeds (Finland), David Soulsby (UK), Sandra Southwell, Walter Spoerle (Germany), Margaret Stack and Peter Munroe, Duncan Taylor, Neil Taylor (UK), Mark Taylor (UK), Emmanuel du Teilhet (France), Diana Valia Chen and Andrew van der Westhuyzen (Australia), Katya Voronicheva (Russia), Julia and Chris Wallace (UK), Elizabeth Watson (UK), Ian Whitby (UK), Jan Wigsten (Mongolia), Felicity Wilcox (UK), Edward Wilson (UK), Andrew Wingham (UK), Jennie Wogan (UK), Rashit Yahin (Russia) and Andrew Young (UK)

Quotations used in Part 5 are from the *Guide to the Great Siberian Railway 1900*. Background information for Vladimir, Suzdal and Nizhny Novgorod was written by Athol Yates and updated from material originally published in *Russia by Rail* (Bradt Guides).

The author and publisher have tried to ensure that this guide is as accurate and up to date as possible but things change quickly in Russia. If you notice any changes or omissions please write to Bryn Thomas at Trailblazer (address on p2) or email him (bryn.thomas@trailblazer-guides.com). A free copy of the next edition will be sent to persons making a significant contribution.

Cover photograph: A rare picture, taken in the early 1970s, of the Trans-Siberian being hauled by a steam engine (© Ron Ziel).

CONTENTS

PART 4: CITY GUIDES AND PLANS

INTRODUCTION

After the classic film of Boris Pasternak's love story, *Dr Zhivago*, there can be few people unaware of the magic of crossing Russia and the wild forests and steppes of Siberia on the longest railway journey in the world, the Trans-Siberian. The distances spanned are immense: almost 6000 miles, a seven-day journey, between Moscow and the Pacific port of Vladivostok (for boat connections to Japan); just under 5000 miles, five days, between Moscow and Beijing.

Since a rail service linking Europe with the Far East was established at the turn of the 19th century, foreign travellers and adventurers have been drawn to it. Most of the early travellers crossed Siberia in the comfort of the carriages of the Belgian Wagon Lits company, as luxurious as those of the Venice-Simplon Orient Express of today. Things changed somewhat after the Russian Revolution in 1917 as it became increasingly difficult for foreigners to obtain permits for Siberia. It was not until the 1960s that the situation improved and Westerners began to use the railway again for getting to Japan, taking the boat from Nakhodka (it now leaves from Vladivostok) for the last part of the journey. In the early 1980s, travel restrictions for foreigners visiting China were eased and now many people have found the Trans-Siberian a fascinating and cheap way to get to or from both the Middle Kingdom and Mongolia.

Rail travel is not only far more environmentally friendly than flying but inevitably passengers absorb something of the ethos of the country through which they travel: on this train you are guaranteed to meet local people, for this is no 'tourist special' but a working service; you may find yourself draining a bottle of vodka with a Russian soldier, discussing politics with a Chinese academic or drinking Russian champagne with a Mongolian trader.

Russia is undergoing phenomenal changes after decades of stagnation. While the ending of the Cold War may have removed some of the mystique of travelling in the former USSR, Russia's increasing accessibility means that there are new travel opportunities right across the country. With foreigners no longer obliged to stay in overpriced state-run hotels, visiting the country is more affordable than ever before.

Although travel in Siberia today presents few of the dangers and difficulties that it did earlier in the last century, a journey on the Trans-Siberian still demands a considerable planning and preparation. Now in its seventh edition with even more detailed information than its predecessors, this book helps you cut through the red tape when arranging the trip, gives background information on Russia and Siberia, and provides a kilometre-by-kilometre guide to the entire route of the greatest rail adventure – the Trans-Siberian.

PLANNING YOUR TRIP

Routes and costs

'Best of all, he would tell me of the great train that ran across half the world ... He held me enthralled then, and today, a life-time later, the spell still holds. He told me the train's history, its beginnings ... how a Tzar had said, 'Let the Railway be built!' And it was ... For me, nothing was ever the same again. I had fallen in love with the Traveller's travels. Gradually, I became possessed by love of a horizon and a train which would take me there ...'

Lesley Blanch *Journey into the Mind's Eye*

ROUTE OPTIONS

Travellers crossing Siberia have a choice of three main routes: the Trans-Siberian, Trans-Manchurian and Trans-Mongolian. The Trans-Siberian is the most expensive route as it crosses the entire length of Siberia to the Pacific terminus at Vladivostok. The Trans-Manchurian travels through most of Siberia before turning south through Manchuria and ending in Beijing. The Trans-Mongolian also terminates in Beijing but travels via Mongolia which gives you the chance to stop off in Ulan Bator.

If you want to travel on to Japan after your trip you have several options. From Vladivostok there are ferries (mid-May to December) and flights. There are also cheaper ferry services from various Chinese ports including Shanghai, Tianjin and Qingdao, all of them within easy reach of Beijing.

Trans-Manchurian and Trans-Mongolian travellers can continue from Beijing by train round China, which has an extensive rail system and also direct rail links into Vietnam. You can even travel back to Europe along the Silk Road on the Turkestan–Siberia (Turksib) railway.

COSTS

Overall costs

How much you pay for a trip on the world's longest railway line depends on the level of comfort you demand, the number of stops you wish to make along the way and the amount of time you're prepared to put into getting hold of a budget ticket.

Although the cheapest tickets for rail travel between Moscow and Beijing (and purchased in these cities) currently cost around £160 (US$310/€230), this does not reflect what you'll end up paying for your trip. Among other big costs to factor in are transport to your departure point, transport back at the end of your journey, accommodation in Moscow, Beijing and any stopover towns, and of course food. If you want to buy your own tickets en route you must budget for the extra time that this will take. In this light the independent package deals

The Longest Journey

If it's a long-distance rail-travel record you're after, begin your journey in Vila Real de Santo António in southern Portugal, cross Europe to Moscow, take the Trans-Mongolian route from there to Beijing and continue to Ho Chi Minh City (Saigon) in Vietnam – a journey of 17,852km (11,155 miles).

For an even longer journey you'll have to wait until the proposed 103km tunnel under the Bering Strait goes ahead. If it really does you'll be able to travel all the way from London to Mexico City via Moscow, Irkutsk, Magadan, Fairbanks and Vancouver – approximately 25,500km (16,000 miles).

offered by many travel agents can be better value than they might appear. Packages on the Trans-Siberian between Moscow and Beijing, including transfers and one night's accommodation in Moscow, start at about £360/US$700.

One-way flights from London cost around £180 to Moscow or £270 to Beijing. The cheapest fully inclusive Trans-Siberian holidays cost from around £1300 including flights to and from London.

From New York, one-way flights cost around US$450-700 to Moscow or US$450-1000 to Beijing, depending on the season. The cheapest fully inclusive Trans-Siberian holidays cost from around US$2500 per person in high season, including flights to and from New York.

From Australia, single flights cost around A$1400 to Beijing or A$1500 to Moscow, depending on the season. The cheapest fully inclusive Trans-Manchurian trip costs around A$3200 per person including two nights in Moscow. A 10-day Vladivostok to Moscow budget package costs from about A$3400 with flights.

If a super-luxurious two-week guided rail tour from Moscow to Vladivostok with en suite accommodation in private saloon cars pulled by a restored steam locomotive is more your idea of travelling, be prepared to part with around £5000/US$10,000 (see p25).

Communist-era travel in Russia

Travel in Russia is much better value and far less restricted than it was in the communist era. It's now easier to get a visa (see p18) and relatively easy to travel independently. You are no longer obliged to deal with state-run travel agencies and you needn't pre-book hotel rooms. Train tickets are easy to buy on your own, although long-distance tickets can still be problematic in the summer season. Still, it's useful to know a bit about how tourism worked in the Soviet Union, because some attitudes and even organizations from that era endure today.

In Soviet times all travel arrangements for foreigners were handled by the monolithic organizations of Intourist (general travel), Sputnik (youth travel) and CCTE (business travel). All charged monopoly prices, and travellers' options were restricted. In the 1990s these organizations were broken up and the travel market opened up. There are still Sputnik offices in many cities. Mainly they book budget transport for Russian students, although they can be useful to foreigners for information and, in some cases, cheap transport and accommodation.

Intourist was the real giant. Most foreign travellers in the country had to book rooms and tours through them. Today, outside the capital, where it still has a faint presence, Intourist is almost extinct. Some hotels built in the communist era still say 'Intourist', but they're now privately owned and most have official-ly taken the word out of their name. Many locals, and even the owners of some small hotels, mistakenly believe that the former Intourist places are still the only hotels that can accept foreigners. They will invariably try to send you there. Likewise, the old Intourist travel desks, which used to be in all the big hotels, have been all but wiped out by lean young Russian and foreign travel agencies.

Accommodation costs

The price and value of accommodation in Russia varies wildly. As a foreigner, you'll sometimes be offered the most expensive rooms first, so get in the habit of asking for something cheaper.

Moscow and St Petersburg are the only places with genuinely five-star hotels (US$400/£200/€300 or more per night) although a number of Trans-Siberian cities, including Khabarovsk and Vladivostok, have good four-star places. Hotel prices in Moscow and St Petersburg are higher than anywhere else in the country.

Most visitors still stay in former Intourist hotels, paying US$40-100/£20-50/€30-80 for a single or US$60-140/£30-70/€45-105 for a double with attached bathroom. Independent travellers who search out basic rooms in cheap-er hotels can expect to pay US$14-40/£7-20/€10-30 for a single or US$16-50/£8-25/€12-40 for a double. Breakfast is sometimes included in the price.

Hostels and guest-houses have sprung up in Moscow, St Petersburg and Irkutsk, charging about US$25-40/£11-20/€16-30 for bed and breakfast.

Not the Trans-Siberian Express!
Travel writers often wax lyrical about the fabled 'Trans-Siberian Express' but in fact no **regular** train service of that name exists. While the British generally refer to their trains by a time (eg 'the 10:35 to Clapham'), the Russians and Chinese identify theirs by a number (eg 'Train No 3' from Beijing to Moscow). As in other countries a few crack services have been singled out and given names, but 'Trans-Siberian Express' is not among them. 'Trans-Siberian', 'Trans-Mongolian' and 'Trans-Manchurian' are, however, common terms for the main **routes** across Siberia and between Moscow and Beijing.

The train which runs all the way from Moscow to Vladivostok is the No 2, and going in the other direction it's the No 1; both services are also called the 'Rossiya'. The No 20 covers the full Trans-Manchurian route from Moscow to Beijing, while in the other direction it's the No 19; these are both called the 'Vostok'. Trains on the Trans-Mongolian route between Moscow and Beijing, and most other long-distance services, are identified only by number.

There is, however, now a luxurious special tourist train that goes by the name of the 'Golden Eagle Trans-Siberian Express' (see p25).

What if I don't want to do it all by train?

Of course you needn't sit in a train for a week to see Siberia or Mongolia. It's quite feasible to fly to or from an intermediate point and travel only part of the way by rail.

Major airports along the Trans-Siberian which have nonstop air connections with Moscow, Beijing or other international hubs include:

Yekaterinburg (Moscow daily from US$160, Frankfurt three times weekly, Prague and Cologne weekly)

Novosibirsk (Moscow daily from US$170, Frankfurt and Hanover almost daily in summer from US$500, Beijing via Shenyang three times weekly from US$370, Seoul weekly from US$500)

Irkutsk (Moscow daily from US$310, Niigata weekly from US$550, Ulan Bator weekly from US$250, and Tianjin, Shenyang and Dalian weekly from US$450)

Vladivostok (Moscow daily from US$420, Harbin weekly from $210, Seoul three times a week from US$420, Osaka weekly from US$525, Niigata weekly from US$385, Dalian twice a week from US$250 and Hanoi weekly from US$475)

Ulan Bator (Moscow several times weekly from US$480, Beijing almost daily from US$200, Irkutsk three times weekly from US$290, and Tokyo, Osaka and Seoul several times weekly from US$390).

Outbound air tickets are generally easy to buy a few days ahead (but see the following note about the Nadaam Festival).

Trans-Siberian specialist agencies such as those listed on pp24-40 can arrange rail tickets for specific segments, although buying these on arrival is quite feasible and gives you more flexibility to alter your plans. You needn't book more than a day ahead for small segments, but you may need more time for longer ones such as Irkutsk–Moscow. Sleeping berths may be scarce on services not originating in your proposed departure town. From October to April it's easy to book almost any train at short notice.

Possibilities include the No 5/6 Ulan Bator–Moscow, No 9/10 Irkutsk–Moscow, No 23/24 Beijing–Ulan Bator, No 25/26 Novosibirsk–Moscow and No 361/362 Ulan Bator–Irkutsk. Certain services and times get heavily booked – eg those to and from Ulan Bator around the time of Mongolia's Nadaam Festival in mid-July.

Homestays are an option available in most larger Trans-Siberian towns, at about US$30-50/£16-25/€24-36 per person per night including some or all meals.

For more information on accommodation see p67.

Train classes and prices

Most Trans-Siberian train carriages intended for foreigners are classed as either *kupé* (coupé; also called 2nd, hard or tourist class), with four-berth closed compartments; or *SV* (also called 1st or soft class), with comfortable two-berth compartments, sometimes with washbasins.

On Trans-Mongolian train Nos 3/4, however, SV compartments are four-berth and identical in layout to all other services' kupé compartments except a bit wider, so they are poor value. But these trains also have an additional '*de luxe 1st*' class, whose carpeted two-berth compartments have armchairs and attached bathrooms, and are the only ones with showers.

Compartments are not single sex. Foreigners may find themselves sharing with other foreigners if they've booked through an agency that deals mainly with non-Russians. For further details on train classes see p71.

Approximate sample prices (including any booking fees) are shown below for a non-stop, no-frills, single (one-way) journey on each of the main routes across Siberia. They range from the cheapest ticket bought over the counter in Moscow or Beijing to those offered by some Western travel agents.

- **Trans-Siberian route** (Moscow–Vladivostok)
  kupé (2nd) US$350-1400/£180-700/€260-1020
  SV (1st) US$600-2000/£300-1000/€450-1500

- **Trans-Manchurian route** (Moscow–Beijing)
  kupé (2nd) US$450-800/£230-400/€330-580
  SV (1st) US$700-1220/£350-620/€520-900

- **Trans-Mongolian route** (Moscow–Beijing)
  kupé (2nd) US$310-750/£160-370/€230-540
  SV (1st) US$550-950/£275-480/€400-730
  deluxe 1st class US$625-1100/£320-550/€470-800

BREAKING YOUR JOURNEY

Most people will want to break their journey and stop off along the way. This is a good idea not only for the chance to stretch your legs and have a shower but also because some of the places you pass through are well worth exploring. You won't learn much about life in Siberia by looking through a train window, especially if you're sharing a compartment with other foreigners. With the exception of a few military centres, all cities on the Trans-Siberian can be visited. If you're booking through an agency, plan carefully: once you have started on your trip, it's too late to change your itinerary. But if you travel independently you can just buy tickets as you go along, and stop off whenever and wherever you like.

If your trip starts in **Moscow** (see p155) it's usually necessary to spend a night there, although you'd need several days to see the main sights. A side-trip to **St Petersburg** (p132) is highly recommended. At the other end, it's certainly worth spending several days in **Beijing** (p344).

In between there's the 'Golden Ring' city of **Nizhny Novgorod** (p217) and historically rich **Yekaterinburg** (p226). **Novosibirsk** (p246) is the sprawling capital of Western Siberia, **Tomsk** (p255) is an interesting university town and **Krasnoyarsk** (p259) is among the region's most pleasantly situated cities. **Irkutsk** (p265), capital of Eastern Siberia, is 64km from beautiful **Lake Baikal** (p278), the world's deepest freshwater lake; a stay beside the lake is highly recommended. **Ulan Ude** (p289) is worth a stop for the Buddhist monastery nearby, and **Khabarovsk** (p303) is surprisingly pleasant. **Vladivostok** (p312), the brawny home port of Russia's Pacific Fleet, is the eastern railway terminus.

Also recommended for those headed to Beijing is a visit to **Ulan Bator** (p322), the capital of Mongolia. Irkutsk and Ulan Bator are the most popular stopovers for Trans-Siberian travellers.

PLANNING YOUR TRIP

When to go

The mode of life which the long dark nights of winter induce, the contrivances of man in his struggle with the climate, the dormant aspect of nature with its thick coverage of dazzling snow and its ice-bound lakes now bearing horses and the heaviest burdens where ships floated and waves rolled, perhaps only a fortnight ago: – all these scenes and peculiar phases of life render a journey to Russia very interesting in winter.
Murray's *Handbook for Travellers in Russia, Poland and Finland* (1865)

For most people 'Siberia' evokes a picture of snowy scenes from the film *Dr Zhivago*, and if they are not to be disappointed, winter is probably the best time to go. It is, after all, the most Russian of seasons, a time of fur coats, sleigh-rides and chilled vodka. In sub-zero temperatures, with the bare birch and fir trees encased in ice, Siberia looks as one imagines it ought to – a barren, desolate

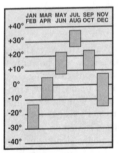

Irkutsk – temperature (average max/min °C)

wasteland (the train, however, is well heated). Russian cities, too, look best and feel most 'Russian' under a layer of snow. St Petersburg with its brightly painted Classical architecture is far more attractive in the winter months when the weather is crisp and skies clear. But if you want to spend time in any Siberian city you'll find it more enjoyable to go in late spring, summer or autumn, when there is more to do.

In Siberia the heaviest snowfalls and coldest temperatures – as low as minus 40°C (minus 40°F) in Krasnoyarsk and some other towns the train passes through – occur in December and January. From late January to early April the weather is generally cold and clear. Spring comes late. In July and

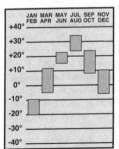

Moscow – temperature (average max/min °C)

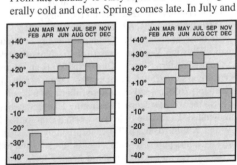

Ulan Bator – temperature (average max/min °C)

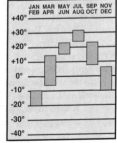

Beijing – temperature (average max/min °C)

> **Winter travel**
> 'I've just got back from a round-the-world journey that began with a trip on the Trans-Siberian Railway. We knew what to look out for, were informed about what we were seeing and, to a certain extent, had an idea of what to expect. Nothing, though, could really prepare one for the pleasure of seeing acres of snow, the tracks going seemingly nowhere, the groups of trees, the delicate reeds and huge frozen rivers and lakes'.
> **Elizabeth Watson** (UK)

August it is warm enough for an invigorating dip in Lake Baikal. The birch and aspen provide a beautiful autumnal display in September and October.

In Moscow the average temperature is 17°C (63°F) in summer and minus 9°C (+16°F) during the winter; there are occasional heavy summer showers.

Tourist season

The tourist season runs from May through September, peaking from mid-July to early September. In the low season, between October and April, some companies offer discounts on tours; you'll also find it much easier to get a booking for the train at short notice at this time. During the summer it can be difficult to get a place on the popular Moscow–Beijing route without planning several weeks ahead.

Bookings and visas

ORGANIZED TOURS OR INDIVIDUAL ITINERARIES?

Note that regulations governing the issuing of Russian visas are particularly susceptible to change. Check the latest situation with your embassy or through the organizations listed on p19.

Group tours

Many visitors come to Russia in organized groups. This is still how the Russian authorities would prefer you to travel: groups are easier to control and tend to spend more money than itinerant backpackers. Going with a tour group certainly takes much of the hassle out of the experience, but it also means there isn't much room for doing your own thing. Most tours are accompanied by an English-speaking guide from the moment you set foot in the country until the moment you leave. See pp24-40 for information on tour companies.

Semi-independent travel

This is the easiest and most popular way for foreigners to travel on the Trans-Siberian. A specialist agency makes all accommodation and train bookings (with or without stops along the way), providing you in the process with the documentation needed for obtaining a Russian tourist visa. You choose departure dates and number and length of stops, in effect designing your own trip. Once in Russia you're usually on your own, although some agencies offer guides to meet you at the station and help you organize your time in stopover cities. You'll often get good quality accommodation in Moscow as part of the deal. Numerous travel agents in the West can make these arrangements (see pp24-40), or you can deal directly with locally based Trans-Siberian specialists such as The Russia Experience (see p24) who have a member of staff in Moscow, or Monkey Business Infocenter in Beijing (see p38).

Fully independent travel

Travelling independently is not difficult and is the best way to gain an insight into the 'real' Russia. Nevertheless many Russians seem baffled by the notion of making up your itinerary as you go along!

Getting a tourist or business visa allows you to wander around freely. For a tourist visa, together with your visa application you must present confirmation of hotel bookings, furnished by a registered Russian tourist organization. Various hotels and agencies can do this for you (see p21). Some will furnish documentation of accommodation for the duration of your visa, in exchange for your booking only your first night's stay with them. Once you have your visa and are registered with the organization that's sponsoring you, or one of their affiliates, you are free to travel wherever you want, irrespective of what the documentation says.

Although few Russians outside the largest cities speak English and the tourist infrastructure is limited, this shouldn't put you off. Many Russians are friendly and generous, and learning a bit of basic Russian before you go will help communication.

ROUTE PLANNING

Main services

The table opposite is a summary of some major Siberian train services. For time-tables and other details see pp450-8, but note that timetables are subject to change, nowhere more so than in this part of the world. There may be occasional one-hour variations on account of differences between countries in implementing Daylight Savings Time. Local times are given opposite but note that official Russian timetables use Moscow Time only.

The trains that run across Siberia are not tourist specials but working services used by local people, and they're very popular. On most routes they run to capacity, especially in summer (when additional services may be laid on). Buying tickets as you go along shouldn't be too difficult, as Russians usually leave it to the last minute. If you book a day before you want to travel, you'll probably get what you want on the smaller sections, but you'll need more time if you want a ticket for the whole route or for a longer section such as Irkutsk–Moscow.

Train	Leaves	on	at	Arrives	on	at
1, *Rossiya*	Vladivostok	Even-no days	21:35	Moscow	Day 7	17:43
2, *Rossiya*	Moscow	Odd-no days	21:25	Vladivostok	Day 8	08:03
3 (Mongolia)	Beijing	Wed	07:45	Moscow	Mon	14:28
4 (Mongolia)	Moscow	Tue	21:35	Beijing	Mon	14:04
5	Ulan Bator	Tue, Fri	13:50	Moscow	Sat, Tue	14:28
6	Moscow	Wed, Thu	21:35	Ulan Bator	Mon, Tue	07:30
9 *Baikal*	Irkutsk	Even-no days	16:15	Moscow	Day 4	16:42
10 *Baikal*	Moscow	Odd-no days	23:25	Irkutsk	Day 5	09:16
19 *Vostok* (Manchuria)	Beijing	Sat	22:56	Moscow	Fri	17:57
20 *Vostok* (Manchuria)	Moscow	Fri	23:55	Beijing	Thu	05:20
23*	Beijing	Tue	07:40	Ulan Bator	Wed	13:20
24*	Ulan Bator	Thu	08:05	Beijing	Fri	14:35
361/363	Ulan Bator	Daily	18:40	Irkutsk	Day 3	07:58
362/364	Irkutsk	Daily	21:00	Ulan Bator	Day 3	07:05

additional service in summer only, dep Beijing (No 23) Mon, Ulan Bator (No 24) Sat

Moscow to Vladivostok

There are many trains on the line between Moscow and Vladivostok, but the famous No 1/2 *Rossiya* train is the top choice for service. Other very good trains which cover shorter segments include the No 9/10 *Baikal* between Moscow and Irkutsk; these increase your options if you are making stopovers along the way.

There are ferries from Vladivostok to Japan and Korea in the summer months (see p321), but increasing numbers of travellers are opting for the cheaper alternative of ferry crossings from various ports in China (see p37).

Moscow to Beijing: Trans-Manchurian or Trans-Mongolian?

You have two route choices between Moscow and Beijing: the Trans-Mongolian route via Ulan Bator in Mongolia, and the Trans-Manchurian route via Harbin in China. There are advantages and disadvantages with each.

The Trans-Manchurian train is the No 19/20 *Vostok*. This currently departs from Beijing at a more civilized time (in the evening) than the Trans-Mongolian (crack of dawn) but costs a bit more. The Moscow departure is in the afternoon for the Trans-Mongolian and in the evening for the Trans-Manchurian.

The Trans-Mongolian Moscow–Beijing service is the No 3/4, although there are additional, shorter-distance options including the No 23/24 (Beijing–Ulan Bator) and No 361/363 and 362/364 (Irkutsk–Ulan Bator). Only the No 3/4 offers de luxe 1st class carriages (see p119), although travellers who opt for kupé will find these carriages identical on both routes. Unless you're American or Israeli you need a Mongolian transit visa on this route, even if you do not stop along the way. The Trans-Mongolian journey takes about 12 hours less than the Trans-Manchurian.

Despite long-standing Trans-Siberian lore, there's no difference between the restaurant cars on the two routes as these are supplied by the country through which you're travelling.

Both trains have weekly departures in each direction. Summer is the most difficult time to book a place on long-distance trains on either route, so make arrangements several months in advance.

Stopping off in Mongolia

If you're taking the Trans-Mongolian route, breaking your journey in Ulan Bator is highly recommended. It's easy to organize either through a specialist agency or independently.

A related option, though not in Mongolia, is a stop at Hohhot (Huhehot) in China's Inner Mongolia province, where you'll find a similar rural Mongolian Buddhist culture and similar grassland tours.

Side trips

There are numerous possibilities for side trips by rail, including on the **Siberian BAM Railway** (from Tayshet) and the **Turksib Railway** (from Novosibirsk), with links via the Turksib to the **Kazakhstan–China Railway**. See p130 for more on all these lines.

From **Blagoveshchensk** (see p407), on a spur off the Moscow–Vladivostok line at Belogorsk, you can cross the Amur River by boat to Heihe in China. With onward connections via Harbin, this little-known alternative to the Trans-Manchurian line is actually the cheapest land route from Moscow to Beijing at present.

A branch line runs from Sibirtsevo, near Vladivostok, via Ussurisk to Pyongyang in **North Korea**, although at the moment such a journey is hard to organize. Russia is keen to foster the extension of this line into South Korea and its deep-water port at Pusan, tying the Trans-Siberian into a potentially very profitable Asia–Europe network.

From Beijing it's easy to continue by rail into **Vietnam**, a three-night journey.

VISAS

Visas are required of most foreigners visiting Russia, Mongolia and China. Getting a Russian visa is not always straightforward (largely because of the need to obtain an invitation and confirmation of your accommodation, if you go for a tourist visa). It's simple to get a Chinese visa from most embassies, and relatively easy to get a Mongolian visa. Visa regulations change regularly; even border guards and local police officials don't always know the latest. Check with travel agents or embassies.

Whether you're starting your trip in Beijing, or Moscow, it's definitely best to get your onward visa for Russia or China elsewhere. The Chinese embassy in Moscow is notoriously difficult to deal with and, officially, the Russian consulate in Beijing issues tourist visas only to residents of China.

You'll always need to show your visa in Russia when staying at a hotel and whenever you buy a rail ticket.

Russia visa invitations

To get a tourist visa to Russia, you must first obtain an invitation or equivalent document (*podtverzhdenie* подтверждение) confirming your accommodation details while in Russia, plus one or more vouchers (*order* ордер) confirming payment for this accommodation. These documents may only be issued by travel agencies, hotels or other organizations registered to do so with the Russian Ministry of the Interior. The documents must all state your passport details, itinerary and duration of stay, along with the inviting organization's address and registration number. If you're going on a package tour, your travel agent will organize everything and you'll see very little of this paperwork.

Although an itinerary must be specified, the visa doesn't list your proposed destinations, allowing independent travellers to visit places on the spur of the moment. Most travel companies will issue an invitation/confirmation only for the days for which you have paid to stay with them, but some will confirm accommodation for the duration of your visa in exchange for your booking just your first night's stay with them, leaving you free to go where you like after that.

Costs for **documentation** in support of a one-month tourist visa (**not** for the visa itself, although the price may include registration of the visa upon arrival: see p22) are approximately US$30-60/£16-33/€30-45 (single entry) or US$45-70/£24-38/€45-60 (double entry).

Tourist visas in Russia are granted only for up to one month. If you want to stay longer you'll need to apply for a business visa or another type of visa. Support for a three-month business visa costs about US$65-165/£41-54/€60-130. Costs in support of multiple-entry business visas will be higher still.

Following are some of the companies that can issue you an invitation, though terms and conditions may vary. All are either Russia based or have offices in Russia. Most hostels and hotels in Moscow (see pp180-1) and St Petersburg (see p149) offer visa support.

• **St Petersburg International Hostel** (☎ +7-812-329 8018, 🖷 +7-812-329 8019, 🖳 www.ryh.ru), ul 3rd Sovietskaya 28, St Petersburg 193036.
• **The Russia Experience** see p24.
• **Monkey Business** see p38.
• **Host Families Association** (HOFA; 🖳 www.hofa.ru), 3 Linia, 6, VO, St Petersburg 199053, Russia. This is a network of academic and professional families offering homestays, flat rental and budget hotels in some 60 Russian cities and elsewhere in the region. See p68 for further details.
• **Real Russia** see p24.
• **Russian Passport** see p34.
• **Travel Directors** see p34.
• **G&R International** (☎ +7-495-378 0001, 🖷 +7-495-378 2866, 🖳 www.hostels.ru), 5th Floor, Zelenodolskaya 3/2, the affiliate of G&R Hostel in Moscow.
• **UniFest Travel** (visa department ☎ +7-495-234 6999, 🖷 +7-495-234 6556, 🖳 www.unifest.ru), Komsomolsky prospekt 13, Moscow 119146.
• **Hostel Sherstone** (☎/🖷 +7-495-783 3438, 🖳 www.sherstone.ru), Gostinichny proezd 8, korpus 1, room 324, Moscow 127106.
• **VisaToRussia.com** (☎ +7-495-956 4422, 🖷 +7-495-956 2244, 🖳 www.visatorussia.com), Leninsky pr 29, offices 401-408, Moscow 117912.
• **Russian Visa Express** (☎ +7-495-545 8690, 🖷 +7-495-955 4279, 🖳 www.visaru.com), 2 Stasovoy ul, Moscow 119991.

Russian visa

A Russian visa is a one-page form stuck directly into your passport, containing your passport information, entry and exit dates, and the name and registration of the organization that has invited you.

Application is normally made at the nearest Russian embassy or consulate. In addition to a completed visa application form you'll be asked for your passport (preferably a 10-year passport, in good condition and with two facing blank pages), invitation/confirmation document, accommodation voucher(s), one to three passport-sized photos and the visa fee. Some embassies will accept faxed copies of visa-support documents, but not all, so check before you apply and don't take your 'host's' word on this.

If you're starting your trip in Beijing you're better off getting your visa at home than doing it in China. At the time of writing, the Russian consulate in Hong Kong was the only Russian consulate in China that would officially accept visa applications from non-residents of China. It was also the only one that would accept faxed or printed copies of invitations or other support documents. Someone else can deliver your documents to the Hong Kong consulate and apply for you, but there must be a Hong Kong entry stamp in your passport.

Other Russian consulates in China would in fact make exceptions and accept foreigners if the consulate wasn't too busy, but only if the applicant had original copies of their invitations and other paperwork from Russia. These are either timely or costly to obtain by post. Transit visas, good for up to 10 days, were still possible to obtain at the Beijing consulate, but you must show your train ticket, and most likely onward visas and tickets as well.

Any foreigner visiting Russia for more than three months requires a doctor's certification that they are not HIV-positive, a requirement introduced to placate anti-West forces in Russia.

The visa fee depends on where you apply (and sometimes on your nationality), the type and duration of the visa, and how quickly you want it. For Americans a visa costs from US$100, for British nationals from £45, and for EU citizens (except those from Denmark and Ireland) from £25, although you can usually get faster service by paying more.

● **Tourist visa** Tourist visas are issued for up to one month, with single-entry and double-entry versions. A tourist visa requires an invitation and a hotel booking, but to secure the invitation this may be for as little as just one night.

● **Business visa** A business visa allows you to stay for up to a year, though not for longer than six months at a stretch without leaving the country, even if it is just for a day. It requires an invitation from a registered Russian business, which is easy enough to get if you use an online visa-support service such as Russian Visa Express and VisatoRussia.com (see p19). Business visas are actually easier to arrange than tourist visas, because you don't need to book accommodation. They're ideal for travellers who want a longer stay in Russia, and many tourists use them, but they are slightly more expensive to obtain than a tourist visa.

● **Private visa** This visa is for foreigners who are invited by Russian friends or relatives, but it can take three months or more to get. The process involves your Russian friend getting an authorization (*izveshchenia* извещение) from their home-town OViR/PVU (Passport & Visa Unit) office and mailing it to you. You must then take it to your Russian embassy, which confirms it with OViR/PVU back in Russia. You can get a private visa for a stay of up to three months, single-entry only. Non-Russian friends in Russia cannot invite you.

● **Transit visa** Transit visas are normally given only to those who are in transit through Russia and not staying overnight in any city. Most Russian embassies issue transit visas for only 72 hours; Russian embassies and consulates in China, however, will issue them for up to 10 days which allows you to travel on the Trans-Siberian, stay in Moscow for a night and then leave. You will probably have to show your Russian rail ticket, and sometimes your onward ticket, when applying for the visa. If you intend to stay anywhere other than Moscow you must get a tourist visa.

Russian visa extension In any country it's always best to arrive with a visa that is certain to cover the length of your stay, rather than having to go to the trouble of extending it.

The situation with visa extensions changes all the time. Provided you have registered your visa (see below), it's possible to get a visa extension but currently not easy. The organization which issued your visa invitation must submit an official request for an extension.

Sometimes an international train ticket is all the proof you need. It's wise to take your original visa invitation and at least three passport photos with you in case you have to extend or replace your visa.

Russian visa registration All visitors staying in Russia for more than 72 hours must register their visas with the local police or OViR/PVU (Passport & Visa Unit) within three business days of arrival, weekends and state holidays excluded. Also, in a relatively new requirement aimed at cracking down on internal migration and terrorism, you must register within three business days in any town where you stay longer than three business days.

You could go to the local OViR/PVU office and do this yourself, but the process can be extremely difficult or impossible to navigate if you don't speak

---

Health insurance
Citizens of countries signatory to the Schengen Convention (Austria, Belgium, Denmark, Finland, France, Germany, Greece, Iceland, Italy, Luxembourg, Netherlands, Norway, Portugal, Spain and Sweden) and from Israel, Estonia and Switzerland who apply for a Russian visa are officially required to produce proof of medical insurance valid in Russia. This is unevenly enforced. Some embassies don't ask at all, others will accept just about any insurance document, while still others insist on coverage by a company having an agreement with Ingosstrakh/Rosno, the Russian state insurance agency.

Russian or take an interpreter. Most hostels and hotels will register you when you check in, stapling a stamped piece of paper to your passport. These can grow into quite a collection. However, many budget hotels either can't or won't register foreigners, and with homestays it almost certainly won't be done.

If the police decide to check your papers (which happens occasionally, especially in train stations) and find that your visa is not registered but it should be, they may fine you. Border officials at your exit point can also fine you for having an unregistered visa, or for conspicuous gaps in registration. Most travellers get off with paying a small amount (around US$30), though far stiffer penalties and even jail time are allowed by law. It pays to keep your train, bus and plane tickets, to prove when you arrived and departed from different places and how long you stayed.

This is still a new requirement, and it's one with some obvious gaps in logic. It's unclear what one should do, for instance, on a rafting trip or hiking in the Altai Mountains. Many small towns and villages lack either an OViR/PVU office or a hotel that can register foreigners. Generally, if you can demonstrate that you made a good-faith effort to follow the rules, officials should be forgiving. The requirement, after all, is meant to control internal migration. Most border guards simply don't bother piecing together travellers' itineraries through Russia and checking it against their registrations when they leave the country.

You should certainly make every effort to register within 72 hours of entering the country. The organization that issued your invitation is expected to handle this, but if you are travelling independently it can be taken care of by staff at your first hotel stop. If the hotel can't or won't do it, take yourself to the nearest OViR/PVU office as soon as you can. There you may have to pay a late-registration fee of a few US dollars, but if you're stopped by an unscrupulous police officer before you do it, you could end up forking out much more, even if three business days have not yet elapsed.

Mongolian visa

Mongolian tourist visas are issued for up to 30 days, and there are single and double-entry versions. A single-entry visa costs around US$30/£40/€25 and takes three or four working days; a quicker service is available for an extra fee. Confusingly, you can also get separate visas for entry and for exit; be certain that your visa is valid for exit too, as the process of getting an endorsement for this once you're in the country is time-consuming.

Transit visas are available for stays of three days and cost from US$15/£35/€20. Embassy officials may ask to see an onward (eg Russian or Chinese) visa.

Mongolia has consular offices along the route of the Trans-Siberian, in Moscow (p177), Irkutsk (p276), Ulan Ude (p293) and Beijing (p350). Visas may also be available at the Mongolian border or at the airport, but it's wise to try and get your visa before you leave home.

The visa is a full-page sticker in your passport. The application process is usually straightforward. You'll need a valid passport, one or two photos and the visa fee. An official letter of invitation from a Mongolian organization or individual is no longer necessary for a transit or 30-day tourist visa, although you'll need one for any visit of more than 30 days.

Americans can stay in Mongolia up to 90 days without a visa, but if they plan to stay longer than 30 days, they must register with the authorities within seven days of arrival. Israelis can stay up to 30 days without a visa.

Mongolian visa extension Many travellers obtain a 30-day extension of their visa in Mongolia, though it can be frustrating. To do this in Ulan Bator, see p331. An extension costs US$2 for each additional day. You can be fined US$80 or more for overstaying your visa.

Mongolian visa registration There is no registration requirement for transit or 30-day tourist visas. If you are staying for more than 30 days you must register with the authorities within seven days of arrival (see p331).

Chinese visa

Tourist visas are generally given for up to a month, although if you apply for a shorter period you may only be granted a visa for the period you request. There are single and double-entry versions, as well as multiple-entry visas for long stays. One-month extensions are easy to arrange in most cities within China, though they're easier in smaller towns where there aren't so many tourists.

The process of getting a visa is straightforward at most Chinese embassies. In addition to your passport and the application form you'll need one photo and the visa fee (eg single/double-entry for £30/45 if obtained from the UK or US$50/75 from the US). Processing usually takes about three working days. Where you are asked on your application to list the places you wish to visit, just write something like Beijing, Shanghai and Guangzhou. It's not checked and doesn't limit you to those places, but is a safer bet than revealing your true intentions (Tibet for example).

If you're planning on entering the country via Russia or Mongolia, try to get your Chinese visa **before** you reach Moscow, as the Chinese embassies in Moscow and Ulan Bator are not easy to deal with.

Other visas

If you are starting from Beijing and planning to continue westward through Europe after you leave Moscow or St Petersburg, depending on your own nationality you may need transit visas for some countries bordering Russia, including Estonia, Latvia, Lithuania, Poland, Belarus or Ukraine. You may find it much easier to get these visas in China than in Moscow; in particular the Ukrainian Embassy in Moscow is notoriously unpredictable and difficult. Try the new Ukrainian consulate in Shanghai; there still isn't one in Beijing.

At the time of writing, nationals of most English-speaking countries needed a visa to visit or transit Belarus and Ukraine. Citizens of EU countries and the US can visit Poland visa-free for up to 90 days (180 days for UK citizens). Nationals of Australia, New Zealand, the USA, Canada and EU countries can visit Estonia, Latvia and Lithuania visa-free.

MAKING A BOOKING IN BRITAIN

The following companies offer Trans-Siberian or more general Russia packages, and some produce their own very informative brochures.

● **The Russia Experience** (☎ 020-8566 8846, ▤ 020-8566 8843, ▱ www.trans-siberian.co.uk – note that the web address is trans-siberian not transsiberian), Research House, Fraser Rd, Perivale, Middlesex UB6 7AQ. Recommended specialists in budget and medium-priced travel for individuals. Their innovative system of guides ('buddies') is popular: if there are places you want to visit they'll take you there, if you want to sit in a bar all day they'll happily sit with you. Homestays can be arranged in most cities, as well as in Siberian villages or Mongolian yurts. They offer a variety of packages, eg Moscow to Beijing with two nights' accommodation in Moscow from £509, or Moscow to Vladivostok, from £570. They also offer trekking and rafting in the Altai, trips to Tuva, and Beetroot Backpackers trips (see p179) by bus or train on interesting routes such as Moscow–Blagoveshchensk–Harbin.

● **Regent Holidays UK** (☎ 0117-921 1711, ▤ 0117-925 4866, ▱ www.regent-holidays.co.uk), 15 John St, Bristol BS1 2HR. Recommended by many readers, Regent specialize in independent travel to Russia, Eastern Europe, the Baltic States as well as China, Mongolia, Vietnam, and North and South Korea. Moscow–Beijing tickets via the Trans-Mongolian or Trans-Manchurian route cost from £520; stopover packages at Lake Baikal and in Irkutsk or Ulan Bator are available. Bookings are accepted from outside the UK. They can arrange visas (allow at least six weeks), flights, tours and accommodation.

● **Just Go Russia** (☎ 020-843 43496, ▤ 020-7160 9390, ▱ www.justgorussia.co.uk), Boundary House, Boston Rd, London W7. Offers a variety of Trans-Siberian packages as well as a large number of adventure, eco and cultural tours, language courses and visa support. They also hold monthly seminars about Russia in London.

● **Real Russia** (☎ 020-7100 7370, ▤ 020-7900 3633, ▱ www.realrussia.co.uk), 3 The Ivories, Northampton St, Islington, London N1 2HY. They provide a comprehensive service including booking train tickets, flights, hotels and getting visas. They also have offices in Moscow, Volgograd and St Petersburg.

● **Sundowners** (☎ 020-8877 7660, ▤ 020-8877 9002, ▱ www.sundowners travel.com), Suite 207B, The Business Village, 3-9 Broomhill Rd, London SW18 4JQ, a recommended Australian travel company which offers individual and small group journeys with the emphasis on cultural, adventure, challenging or upmarket travel. The Vodkatrain is a budget-friendly unescorted tour using local guides at stopover towns. Group trips accompanied by a Sundowners group leader throughout include a 14-day Trans-Mongolian trip from Moscow to Beijing from £855 to a 34-day Grand Trans-Mongolian Railway journey from Shanghai to Helsinki from £2520. They can organize flights, visas and accommodation en route.

● **China Travel Service and Information Centre** (CTSIC; ☎ 020-7388 8838, ▤ 020-7388 8828, ▱ www.chinatravel.co.uk), 124 Euston Rd, London NW1

2AL. Friendly staff here can help with tickets from Beijing to Moscow (this direction only) as well as tours throughout China. Prices for Beijing–Moscow start at around £188/222/280 (hard/soft/soft de luxe class) on the Trans-Manchurian or Trans-Mongolian route; Beijing–Ulan Bator costs £89/135 (hard/soft de luxe). You're given a voucher which you exchange in Beijing for a confirmed ticket.

● **Great Rail Journeys Ltd** (☎ 01904-521936, 🖷 01904-521905, 🖥 www.great rail.com), Saviour House, 9 St Saviourgate, York YO1 8NL. This recommended rail-holiday specialist organizes an 18-day excursion from London to Vladivostok using the luxurious 'Golden Eagle Trans-Siberian Express' in Russia (see below). There are stops in Warsaw, Moscow, Kazan, Yekaterinburg, Novosibirsk, Irkutsk and Lake Baikal, Ulan Ude, a side trip to Mongolia (Ulan Bator), and Vladivostok with a flight back to London. The cost is from £6395.

● **Intourist Ltd** has offices in London (☎ 020-7727 4100, 🖷 020-7727 8090, 🖥 www.intourist.co.uk; 7 Wellington Terrace, Notting Hill, London W2 4LW) and Glasgow (☎ 0141-204 5809, 🖷 0141-204 5807; Suite 612, Queens House, 19 St Vincent Place, Glasgow G1 2DT). Intourist Ltd now concentrates on independent travel, and for some reason most of its Trans-Siberian clients book through the Glasgow branch. They'll take care of flights, accommodation, train tickets, transfers, visas and excursions.

● **On the Go** (☎ 020-7371 1113, 🖷 020-7471 6414, 🖥 www.onthegotours .com), 68 North End Rd, London W14 9EP, caters for the budget traveller. Their brochure is comprehensive and filled with useful practical information.

● **Steppes Travel** (☎ 01285-651010, 🖷 01285-885888, 🖥 www.steppestravel .co.uk), The Travel House, 51 Castle St, Cirencester, Glos GL7 1QD, offers tailor-made individual Trans-Siberian itineraries and tours, plus options for Moscow, St Petersburg and the Russian Far East (eg a 16-day Moscow to Beijing itinerary is about £2000, with flights). Even if you stay home, their catalogue is an excellent dream-book.

● **GW Travel Ltd/The Trans-Siberian Express Company** (☎ 0161-928 9410, 🖷 0161-941 6101, 🖥 www.gwtravel.co.uk), Denzell House, Denzell Gardens, Dunham Rd, Altrincham, Cheshire WA14 4QF, runs distinctly upmarket tours on their 'Golden Eagle Trans-Siberian Express', a fully restored private steam train with air-conditioned carriages. This is Russia's version of the Orient Express and there are en suite facilities with power showers for each sleeping compartment, flatscreen DVDs, fine dining and extensive wine lists. A two-week escorted tour from Moscow via St Petersburg to Vladivostok (or vice-versa) costs from £5494 to £9995 (£3895 with shared facilities). There are regular summer departures and occasional winter ones, plus an annual July trip to Ulan Bator for the Naadam festival. Several other agencies also feature their tours.

Budget travellers booking from Britain should note that they can also arrange Trans-Siberian rail tickets through specialist agencies in China (see pp38-40) and Russia (p31).

If it's just a flight-only deal you're looking for check websites such as 🖥 www.cheapflights.co.uk or 🖥 www.expedia.co.uk, or get in touch with a bargain-ticket agency such as **STA Travel** (☎ 0870-160 0599, 💻 www.statrav el.co.uk), **Trailfinders** (☎ 0845-058 5858, 💻 www.trailfinders.com), **Flight Centre** (☎ 0870-499 0040, 💻 www.flightcentre.co.uk) or **Dial A Flight** (☎ 0870-333 4488, 💻 www.dialaflight.com).

Further information Russia has no state tourism office in Britain, although from time to time some travel agent with Moscow links sets itself up as the 'Official Russian Tourist Office' in an effort to sell more of its own tours.

For information on the Chinese section of the journey, visit the **China National Tourist Office** (☎ 020-7373 0888, brochure line ☎ 0900-160 0188, 🖹 020-7373 9989, 💻 www.cnto.org.uk/info/uk.htm), 71 Warwick Rd, London SW5 9HB.

Embassies in Britain The **Russian Embassy** (☎ 020-7229 8027, 🖹 020-7229 3215, visa information service ☎ 020-7499 1029 or ☎ 0906-550 8960, 💻 www.rusemblon.org) is at 5 Kensington Palace Gardens, London W8 4QS; it's open for applications 08:30-12:00 (last application 11:45) Monday to Friday. Queues here can be long, and you may wish to pay for the visa service offered by most Russia-specialist travel agencies (prices vary). Your visa invitation must specify accommodation for all nights you will be in Russia. In order for you to get a visa most of the companies listed on p19 will state on their support documents that you're staying with them for the duration of your trip, even though they know you may not do so. A single-entry tourist visa available in seven working days costs £45 and from £95 for a same-day service. A double-entry visa costs £10 more. For postal applications allow at least three weeks.

The **Mongolian Embassy** (☎ 020-7937 0150, 🖹 020-7937 1117, 💻 www .embassyofmongolia.co.uk) is at 7 Kensington Court, London W8 5DL; the visa section is open 10:00-12:30 Monday to Friday. An entry or transit visa costs £35 (rail confirmation is not required) and a single-entry/exit tourist visa costs £40; visas take two to five working days to process but a same-day service is possible for an additional payment of £20. You'll need one photo.

The **Chinese Embassy** (visa information ☎ 09001-880808 or ☎ 020-7631 1430 on weekdays between 14:00 and 16:00, 🖹 020-7436 9178, 💻 www.chi nese-embassy.org.uk) is at 31 Portland Place, London W1B 1QD; the visa section is open 09:00-12:00 Monday to Friday. A one-month tourist visa is quite easy to obtain yourself and takes four working days unless you pay £20 for the same-day service or £15 for the next day. You'll need one passport photo and the fee of £30/45 (single/double entry). Check the dates on the visa before leaving the embassy. There are **Chinese consulates** in Manchester (☎ 0161-224 8672, 💻 www.manchester.chineseconsulate.org; Denison House, 49 Denison Rd, M14 5RX) and Edinburgh (☎ 0131-337 3220, 💻 www.edinburgh.chi neseconsulate.org; 55 Costorphine Rd, EH12 5QG).

The **Belarus Embassy** (consular section ☎ 020-7938 3677, 🖹 020-7361 0005, 💻 www.ukbelembassy.org/consular.html) is at 6 Kensington Court, London W8 5DL; visa section is open 09:30-12:30 Monday, Tuesday, Thursday and Friday. Phone calls are answered Monday to Friday 14:00-16:00. For the mandatory 48-hour Belarussian transit visa you'll need one photo plus a fee of £44 (five working days) or £79 (48 hours); you may also be asked to show your onward visa. Processing takes five working days.

The **Ukrainian Embassy** (☎ 020-7243 8923, 🖹 020-7727 3567, 🖳 www .mfagov.ua/uk) is at 78 Kensington Park Rd, London W11 2PL; visa section open 09:30-12:00 Monday to Friday. Visas are no longer required by most nationalities for stays of up to 90 days but check before travelling.

Getting to Moscow from Britain

● **By air** Flights to Moscow start at around £140 one-way, £220 return. Aeroflot (☎ 020-7355 2233) offers the cheapest seats most often, all to Sheremetyevo-2 airport. Bmi and Transaero now have daily flights to Moscow Domodedovo from London.

● **By rail** The Man in Seat Sixty-One (🖳 www.seat61.com – see p48) has useful information on the options. Deutsche Bahn Travelservice (☎ 0871-880 8066, 🖹 020-8339 4700, 🖳 www.bahn.co.uk) can book a one-way ticket from London to Moscow for as little as £207 (advance purchase); they also sell return tickets but say the return sleeper bookings are not always honoured in Moscow. The daily train service takes about 44 hours, with train changes in Brussels and Berlin. Tickets to a range of European cities (but not currently in Russia) can be booked through Rail Europe (☎ 08705-837 1371, 🖳 www.raileurope.co.uk) or Eurostar (☎ 08705-186186, 🖳 www.eurostar.com).

Getting to Beijing from Britain

● **By air** Flying to **Beijing** is more expensive: at least £340 one way, £440 return. Air China is a good bet for cheap seats and can be booked through CTSIC or other UK agencies; see pp24-5.

MAKING A BOOKING IN CONTINENTAL EUROPE

From Czech Republic

● **Jason Travel** (☎ 222 710 148, 🖹 222 713 338, 🖳 www.jasontravel.cz), Chelcickeho 13, 130 00 Praha 3. Visas, accommodation, flights and rail tickets.
● **Adventura** (☎ 271 741 734, 🖹 271 741 737, 🖳 www.adventura.cz), Voronezska 20, 101 00 Prague 10, specializes in independent and adventure travel, including Russia and China.

From Denmark

● **Kilroy Travels** (☎ 70 15 40 15, 🖳 www.kilroytravels.dk) is a youth/student agency, with half a dozen branches around the country, which sells Trans-Mongolian and Trans-Manchurian tickets and can arrange visas and flights as well as accommodation in some Russian cities.

From Finland

● **Kilroy Travels** (☎ 0203-545769, 🖳 www.kilroytravels.fi) is a youth-student agency with branches around Finland; see under Denmark for services.
● **OY Finnsov Tours** (☎ 09-436 6960, 🖹 09-436 69620, 🖳 www.finnsov.info), Museokatu 15, 00100 Helsinki, is an Intourist affiliate agency.

From France
● **Adeo** (☎ 01 43 72 80 20, 🖨 01 43 72 79 09, 🖳 www.adeo-voyages.com), 68 boulevard Diderot, 75012 Paris.
● **Inexco Voyages** (☎ 01 47 42 25 95, 🖨 01 47 42 26 95, 🖳 www.inexco.fr), 29 rue Tronchet, 75008 Paris. Inexco is a Switzerland-based agency with expertise in tourism from France to states of the former CIS.
● **Cgtt Voyages** (☎ 0825 16 24 88, 🖨 01 40 22 88 11, 🖳 www.cgtt-voyages.fr), 82 rue d'Hauteville, 75010 Paris: group tours.
● **China Travel Service** (☎ 01 44 51 55 66, 🖨 01 44 51 55 60, 🖳 www.cts-france.com), 32 rue Vignon, 75009 Paris, offers bargain Paris–Beijing airfares and help with China visas. Recommended by readers.
● **Office du Tourisme de Chine** (☎ 01 56 59 10 10, 🖨 01 53 75 32 88, 🖳 www.cnto.org, paris@cnta.gov.cn), 15 rue de Berri, 75008 Paris. This official tourist information office can also help with China visas and air tickets, though not railway bookings.
● **Marsans/Transtours** (☎ 08 25 03 10 34, or ☎ 01 40 17 94 00, 🖨 01 40 17 94 05, 🖳 www.marsans.fr), 49 av de l'Opéra, 75002 Paris. Arrange group tours.

From Germany
● **Travel Service Asia** (☎ 07351-373210, 🖨 07351-373211, 🖳 www.tsa-reisen.de), Schmelzweg 10, 88400 Biberach/Riß. TSA offers a range of independent journeys and budget tours on the Trans-Siberian, Trans-Manchurian and Trans-Mongolian routes, including in Mongolia. Through Baikal Complex in Irkutsk (see p273) they offer Lake Baikal hiking tours. They can also arrange visas and visa support, and are worth contacting even if you don't live in Germany.
● **Lernidee-Erlebnisreisen** (☎ 030-786 0000, 🖨 030-786 5596, 🖳 www.trans siberian-railroad-travel.com, 🖳 www.lernidee.de), Eisenacherstrasse 11, 10777 Berlin. Siberian itineraries range from a 2nd-class ticket on the Moscow–Beijing train to stopovers in Mongolia (three nights including full board, with English-speaking guide). Other routes include Moscow to Vladivostok. Homestay and hotel accommodation are offered in several cities.
● **White Nights** (☎ 0178-475 0566, 🖳 engel@wnights.de, 🖳 www.wnights.com), Winstrasse 17, 10405 Berlin, is the German agent for this St Petersburg-based budget travel operator.
● **Die Bahn** (☎ 01805-996633, 🖳 www.reiseauskunft.bahn.de). With Deutsche Bahn's switched-on, multilingual travel service, you can make Trans-Siberian rail bookings by telephone or online.
● **China Tourist Office** (☎ 069-520135, 🖨 069-528490, 🖳 www.cnto.org, frank furt@cnta.gov.cn), Ilkenhanstrasse 6, D-60433 Frankfurt am Main. The official government tourism information office for Germany, Austria and the Netherlands.

From the Netherlands
● **Tozai Travel** (☎ 020-6262272, 🖨 020-6279736, 🖳 www.tozai.nl), Nieuwezijds Voorburgwal 175, 1012 RK Amsterdam. This agency, recommended by readers, concentrates on itineraries for individual travellers.

Trains from Germany

'It comes as no surprise to those who know some geography that Deutsche Bahn, German Rail, has the best (and oldest) rail connections with Russia. There are several options:

● The old 'Est–West-Express', formerly going Paris–Moscow, still operates Cologne–Moscow as a direct service on Fridays in July and August.

● There is a daily (not Sat and in winter, Wed/Fri/Sun) train from Berlin (departure from Lichtenberg Station) to Moscow; this is the Moskva Express and sleeping cars are attached for the St Petersburg route.

● **Reservations** Ask at any German railway station or at their telesales office for tickets inside Russia and their reaction sounds like you are already in Russia: 'That's impossible!' Well, it's somehow tricky because reservations must not be sold for every train, but with insistence I got myself a ticket for the Moscow–Irkutsk train at Dusseldorf railway station. Also ask for special return offers, eg Cologne–Irkutsk –Cologne for about $350!

Reservation can also be done by phone (☎ +49-1805-996633, speaking some German may be helpful but someone will speak English). You will then get a reservation number: quote this number at any German ticket counter and your reservation will be printed.

● **Information** Linked via the website of Deutsche Bundesbahn (🖳 www.bahn.de), you can simply enter the time and date you want to go from and to. The server knows all European and Russian long-distance trains. English speakers can go to 🖳 www.bahn .co.uk and do the same'.   **Benedikt Jaeger** (Germany)

● **White Nights** (☎ 070-360 7785, 🖳 www.wnights.com), Laan van Heldenburg 26A3, 2271 AT Voorburg, is the Dutch agent for this St Petersburg-based budget travel operator.
● **VNC Travel** (☎ 030-231 1500, 🖷 030-231 0232, 🖳 www.vnc.nl), Catharijnesingel 70, 3500 AB Utrecht, can organize trips for independent travellers as well as group tours.
● **Tiara Tours** (☎ 076-565 28 79, 🖷 076-560 26 30, 🖳 www.tiaratours.nl), Charles Petitweg 35/10, 4827 HJ Breda. This Trans-Sib specialist has a user-friendly website.
● **Eurocult** (☎ 030-243 9634, 🖷 030-244 2475, 🖳 www.eurocult.nl), Wittevrouwenstraat 36, 3512 CV Utrecht, can book Trans-Siberian tickets.
● **Kilroy Travels** (☎ 0900-040 0636, 🖳 www.kilroytravels.nl) have branches in a number of cities and can book Trans-Siberian tickets.

From Norway
● **Kinareiser** (☎ 22-98 22 00, 🖷 22-98 22 01, 🖳 www.kinareiser.no), Hegdehaugsveien 10, 0167 Oslo.
● **Intourist Norway** (☎ 22-42 28 99, 🖷 22-42 62 01, 🖳 www.intourist.no), Fr Nansens Plass 8, 0160 Oslo, can arrange tickets for all routes (in either direction) as well as visas and accommodation.
● **Kilroy Travels** (☎ 026 33, 🖳 www.kilroytravels.no) have branches in a number of cities and can book Trans-Siberian tickets.

Cheap tickets via Poland
'I live in Poland and this information concerning getting to Russia from Poland may be useful for travellers planning to travel to Moscow because all the main routes from Western Europe to Russia cross Poland. If you want to go from Berlin, for example, to Moscow, the cheapest way is not to take international direct trains. Do the journey in stages and take the EuroCity train Berlin–Warsaw (€39.80, $5^1/2$ hours), then the rapid train Warsaw–Terespol (around €5, 3 hours). This city is located right next to the border with Belarus, and on the other side of the River Bug that separates Poland from Belarus is the city of Brest. You can either cross the border by foot or take a train. In Brest you can buy a plastcartny ticket to Moscow ($22) or even buy a ticket for the whole Trans-Siberian route'.

Jacob Pilch (Poland)

From Poland
● **Intourist Warsawa Ltd** (☎ 22-625 0852, 🗎 22-629 0202, 🖥 www .intourist.pl), 10 Nowogrodzka str, 00-509 Warsaw.

From Russia
Many organizations within Russia can arrange visa support (see p19). For others, refer to the travel agents in each city (see Part 4: City Guides and Plans).

Moscow You should have no problem buying short-distance rail tickets a day or two ahead of your chosen departure day. The big exception is with the long-distance Trans-Siberian routes. In summer it's best to buy these as far in advance as possible.

Those with a straightforward itinerary are best off using one of the service centres in the railway stations. They're quick, but the price includes a mark-up of about R100 for each ticketed segment.

The easiest source of tickets is at one of these travel agencies or the travel agent in your hostel or hotel. They will tag on various commission fees, though.
● **Galileo-Rus** (☎ 799 9616, 🖥 train@galileo.ru, www.galileo.ru), pl Kudrinkskaya 1, entrance 7 (metro: Barikadnaya).
● **UniFest Travel** (☎ 234 6999, 🗎 234 6556, 🖥 www.unifest.ru), Komsomolsky pr 13 (metro: Park Kultury).
● **Star Travel** (☎ 797 9555, 🖥 www.star travel.ru), Baltiiskaya ul 9, 3rd floor (metro: Sokol). This student-friendly agency does hotel bookings, air ticketing, and sells international youth and student cards.
● **Intourist** (☎ 956 4519/234 9509, 🖥 info@intourist.ru), pereulok Stoleshnikov 11 (metro: Kuznetsky Most).

To avoid the mark-ups, you can go to one of the **Central Railway Agency's** four offices:
● The east side of Yaroslavsky station (metro: Komsomolskaya)
● Maly Kharitonevsky pereulok 6/11, korpus 2 (metro: Chistye Prudy or Krasnaya Vorota)

- Leningradsky pr 1, in the building across the tracks behind Belorussky station (metro: Belorusskaya)
- Mozhaysky Val ul 4/6 (metro: Kievskaya).

A more frustrating experience is to go to the relevant train station. Note that you can only buy tickets for trains departing from that station.

- **China Embassy (Moscow)** (☎ 143-1543, 🖹 230-7523, ⌨ www.ruchina-embassy.org/rus), ul Druzhby 6, metro Universitet. Open for applications 09:00-11:30 weekdays. You're strongly advised to get your Chinese visa at home, since this consulate is notoriously difficult to deal with. Try to arrive by 07:00; if there are more than 20 people ahead of you it's unlikely you'll get in; consider paying the on-the-spot US$30 express surcharge so you don't have to queue again.
- **Mongolia Embassy (Moscow)** (☎ 241-1458, 🖹 291-6171, ⌨ mongolia@glasnet.ru), Spasopeskovsky pereulok 7, metro Smolenskaya, open for applications 09:00-13:00 weekdays.

St Petersburg Long-distance and international tickets can be purchased from the departure station or from the **Railways Ticket Office** at naberezhnaya Kanala Griboyedova 24. To avoid the crowds, there is a little-used window in the **Central Air Ticket Office** on Nevsky pr 7/9 that sells rail tickets.

From Sweden

- **Eco Tour Production** (☎ 0498 487 105, 🖹 0498 487 115, ⌨ www.nomadicjourneys.com), Norra Kustvägen 17, 620 20 Klintehamn, Gotland, is a Swedish partner with Nomadic Journeys, an Ulan Bator-based tour operator and one of the few locally based consolidators for train tickets. On offer are horse riding, sports fishing, popular *ger* (yurt) camp stays and longer horseback expeditions. Camps are low-impact and quiet, with wind and solar power instead of generators. Eco Tour can also help with train journeys starting from Ulan Bator.
- **Iventus International Travel** (☎ 08-651 4523, 🖹 08-651 2558, ⌨ www.iventustravel.se), Hantverkargatan 32, Box 22064, 104 22 Stockholm, is an outlet for Eco Tour/Nomadic Journeys and a specialist in travel to (and onward from) China. On offer are air, train and ferry bookings; hotels and homestays; Baikal, Ulan Bator and China programmes; and Russia, Mongolia and China visa services.
- **Kilroy Travels** (☎ 0771-545769, ⌨ www.kilroytravels.se) have branches in a number of cities and can book Trans-Siberian tickets.

From Switzerland

- **East-West Gateway/Trans-Siberian Gateway** (☎ 021-803 04 78, ⌨ www.trans-siberian-gateway.com), Espace Est-Ouest Sàrl, Place de la Gare 7, CH-1110 Morges 1. Runs tours and can organize individual rail-only tickets for a wide range of destinations within Russia.
- **White Nights** (☎ 079-549 7806, ⌨ www.wnights.com), Freiburgstrasse 18, 2500 Biel, is the Swiss agent for this St Petersburg-based budget travel operator.

PLANNING YOUR TRIP

MAKING A BOOKING IN NORTH AMERICA

From the USA
● **Adventure Center** (☎ 510-654-1879, 🖨 510-654-4200, 🖳 www.adventure center.com), Suite 200, 1311 63rd Street, Emeryville, CA 94608. Agents for the popular Sundowners Adventure Travel trips (see p34).
● **White Nights** (☎/🖨 916-979-9381, 🖳 www.wnights.com), 610 La Sierra Drive, Sacramento, CA 95864, is the US office of a Russia-based budget travel operator. Moscow to Vladivostok costs from US$410.
● **Mir Corporation** (☎ 206-624-7289, toll-free ☎ 1-800-424-7289, 🖨 206-624-7360, 🖳 www.mircorp.com), 85 South Washington St, Suite 210, Seattle, WA 98104. Mir offer a range of individual and small-group escorted tours on the Trans-Siberian, with homestay or hotel accommodation; they're also the USA agent for the Trans-Siberian Express Company (see p25). They have branch offices in Moscow, St Petersburg, Irkutsk and Ulan Ude.
● **Go to Russia Travel** (☎ 404-827-0099, toll-free ☎ 1-888-263-0023, 🖨 404-827-0435, 🖳 www.gotorussia.net), 309A Peters St, Atlanta, GA 30313. This Russia specialist company offers both individual travel assistance (including flights and visa support) and package tours.
● **Boojum Expeditions** (☎ 406-587-0125, toll-free ☎ 1-800-287-0125, 🖨 406-585 3474, 🖳 www.boojum.com), 14543 Kelly Canyon Rd, Bozeman, MT 59715. Through its office in Ulan Bator (🖳 boojum@mongol.net), Boojum organizes horse-riding trips in Mongolia as well as jeep tours.
● **General Tours** (toll-free ☎ 1-800-221-2216, 🖨 603-357-4548, 🖳 www.gen eraltours.com), 53 Summer St, Keene NH 03431, a venerable agency organizing mainly escorted tours, including on the Trans-Siberian.
● **Sokol Tours** (☎ 1-724-935 5373, 🖳 www.sokoltours.com) can arrange visas, train tickets and book accommodation as well as operating a number of tours.
● **RailsNW** (toll-free ☎ 1-800-717-0108, 🖨 503-297-4543, 🖳 www.rails nw.com), 10200 SW Eastridge St, Suite 210, Portland OR97225, operate tours on the Trans-Siberian.
● **The Society of International Railway Travelers** (toll-free ☎ 800-478-4881, ☎ 502-454-0277, 🖨 502-458-2250, 🖳 www.irtsociety.com), 1810 Sils Ave, Louisville, KY 40205, is a membership organization which organizes de luxe train trips all over the world, including Siberian journeys with the Trans-Siberian Express Company (see p25).

A major budget airfare specialist is **STA Travel** (toll-free ☎ 1-800-781-4040, 🖳 www.statravel.com), with offices all over the country.

You can get information from the **Russian National Tourist Office** (☎ 212-575-3431, toll-free ☎ 1-877-221-7120, 🖳 www.russia-travel.com), 130 West 42nd St, Suite 1804, New York, NY 10036. The **China National Tourist Office** has branches in New York (☎ 212-760-8218, 🖳 www.cnto.org, 350 5th Avenue, Suite 6413, New York, NY 10118) and Los Angeles (☎ 818-545-7507, 🖳 la @cnto.org), 550 N Brand Blvd, Suite 910, Glendale, Los Angeles, CA 91204).

Getting to Russia or China from the USA
Numerous airlines fly from the US to Russia. Aeroflot is among the cheapest, with departures from many US cities. From New York, one-way flights to Moscow cost US$430-700 depending on the season. Aeroflot also flies direct from Seattle to Moscow every day. Korean Air has flights from several west-coast cities via Seoul to Vladivostok. Magadan Airlines (☎ 907-248-2994) operates daily direct flights from Anchorage to Magadan (on Russia's Pacific coast), from where you can fly to major Siberian cities.

One-way flights to Beijing start at about US$450 from New York or US$330 from Los Angeles.

Embassies in the USA The consular office of the **Russian Embassy** (☎ 202-298-5700, 🖹 202-298-5735, 💻 www.russianembassy.org) is at 2650 Wisconsin Ave NW, Washington DC 20007. There are also **consulates** in San Francisco (☎ 415-928-6878, 🖹 415-929-0306, 2790 Green St, CA 94123), New York (☎ 212-348-0926, 🖹 212-831-9162, 11 E 91st St, NY 10128), Seattle (☎ 206-728-1910, 🖹 206-728-1871, 2323 Westin Building, 2001 6th Ave, Seattle, WA 98121) and Houston (☎ 713-337-3300, 🖹 713-337-3305, 1333 West Loop South, Suite 1300, Houston, TX 77027).

The consular office of the **Chinese Embassy** (☎ 202-338-6688, 🖹 202-588-9760, 💻 www.china-embassy.org) is at 2201 Wisconsin Ave NW, Rm 110, Washington DC 20007. There are **consulates** in New York (☎ 212-868-7752, 🖹 212-502-0245, 520 12th Ave, New York, NY 10036), Chicago (☎ 312-803-0098, 🖹 312-803-0122, 100 W Erie St, Chicago, IL 60610), Houston (☎ 713-524-4311, 🖹 713-524-7656, 3417 Montrose Blvd, Houston, TX 77006), Los Angeles (☎ 213-807-8088, 🖹 213-380-1961, 443 Shatto Pl, Los Angeles, CA 90020) and San Francisco (☎ 415-674-2900, 🖹 415-674-0494, 1450 Laguna St, San Francisco, CA 94115).

The **Mongolian Embassy** (☎ 202-333-7117, 🖹 202-298-9227, 💻 www .mongolianembassy.us) is at 2833 M Street NW, Washington DC 20007.

The **Belarus Embassy** (☎ 202-986-1606, 🖹 202-986-1805, 💻 www.bel arusembassy.org) is at 1619 New Hampshire Ave NW, Washington DC 20009. There's a consulate in New York (☎ 212-682-5392, 🖹 212-682-5491, 708 3rd Ave, New York, NY 10017).

From Canada
● **Intours Corp** (☎ 416-766-4720, toll-free ☎ 1-800-268-1785, 🖹 416-766-8507, 💻 www.tourussia.com), 2150 Bloor St West, Suite 308, Toronto, Ontario M6S 1M8. This Intourist affiliate can organize individual or group trips on all Trans-Siberian routes, including arrangements in neighbouring countries.
● **Trek Escapes** (☎ 416-922-7584, toll-free ☎ 1-800-267-3347, 🖹 416-922-8136, 💻 www.trekescapes.com), at 223 Carlton St, Toronto M5A 2L2, is an agent offering a range of individual and group Trans-Siberian itineraries, with branches in Vancouver (toll-free ☎ 1-800-663-5132, 2911 West 4th Avenue, Vancouver V6J 1M4), Edmonton (toll-free ☎ 1-800-387-3574, 8412 109th St,

Edmonton T6G 1E2) and Calgary (toll-free ☎ 1-800-690-4859, 336 14th St NW, Calgary T2N 1Z7).

● **Great Canadian Travel** (☎ 204-949-0199, toll-free ☎ 1-800-661-3830, 💻 www.greatcanadiantravel.com), at 158 Fort St, Winnipeg, MB R3C 1C9, can book flights and offer a 15-day tour on the Trans-Siberian.

● **Travel CUTS/Voyages Campus** (toll-free ☎ 1-866-246-9762, 💻 www.travelcuts.com) is Canada's best bargain-ticket agency, with offices countrywide.

The **China National Tourist Office** (☎ 416-599-6636, 🖨 416-599-6382, 💻 www.tourismchina-ca.com) is at 480 University Ave, Suite 806, Toronto, Ontario M5G 1V2.

Embassies in Canada The consular department of the **Russian Embassy** (☎ 613-236-7220, 🖨 613-238-6158, 💻 www.rusembcanada.mid.ru) is at 52 Range Rd, Ottawa, Ontario K1N 8J5. There are **consulates** in Montreal (☎ 514-842-5343, 🖨 514-842-2012) at 3685 Ave du Musée, Montreal, Quebec H3G 2E1, and in Toronto (☎ 416-962-9911, 🖨 416-962-6611) at 130 Bloor St West, Suite 700, Toronto, Ontario M5S 1N5.

The **Chinese Embassy** (☎ 613-789-3434, 🖨 613-789-1911, 💻 www.chinaembassycanada.org) is at 515 St Patrick St, Ottawa, Ontario K1N 5H3. There are **consulates** in Vancouver (☎ 604-736-5188, 🖨 604-737-0154, 3380 Granville St, Vancouver, BC V6H 3K3), Toronto (☎ 416-964-7260, 🖨 416-324-6468, 240 St George St, Toronto, Ontario M5R 2P4) and Calgary (☎ 403-537-1247, 🖨 403-264-6656, 1011 6th Ave, Suite 100, Calgary, Alberta T2P 0W1).

The **Mongolian Embassy** (☎ 613-569-3830, 🖨 613-569-3916, 💻 www.mongolembassy.org) is at 151 Slater St, Suite 503, Ottawa K1P 5H3.

The **Belarus Embassy** (☎ 613-233-9994, 🖨 613-233-8500, 💻 belamb@igs.net) is at 130 Albert St, Suite 600, Ottawa K1P 5G4.

MAKING A BOOKING IN AUSTRALASIA

From Australia
● **Travel Directors** (☎ 08-9242 4200, toll-free ☎ 1-800-641236, 🖨 08-9242 5366, 💻 www.traveldirectors.com.au), 177 Oxford St, Leederville, Perth, WA 6007. This recommended Trans-Siberian specialist agency offers high-quality tour packages strong on person-to-person contact, along with basic visa support.

● **Russian Passport** (☎ 03-9867 3888, 🖨 03-9820 0802, 💻 www.travelcentre.com.au), Suite 11, 401 St Kilda Rd, Melbourne, Victoria, 3004.

● **Sundowners Adventure Travel** (☎ 03-9672 5300, 🖨 03-9672 5311, 💻 www.sundownerstravel.com), Suite 15, 600 Lonsdale St, Melbourne, Vic 3000, is recommended by several readers. They offer both independent and group Trans-Siberian, Trans-Mongolian and Trans-Manchurian trips. Sample group trips include a 19-day St Petersburg to Vladivostok journey including 11 nights in hotels and guesthouses. Under the name Vodkatrain (💻 www.vodkatrain.com) they also offer loosely structured, unescorted group journeys for people aged 18-35, with young local guides at stopover towns.

● **On The Go** (☎ 1300-855684, 🖳 www.onthegotours.com), 3/690 Brunswick St, New Farm, Brisbane, QLD 4005 See p24.
● **Russian Travel Centre/Eastern Europe Travel** (☎ 02-9262 1144, 🖺 02-9262 4479, 🖳 www.eetbtravel.com), Level 5, 75 King St, Sydney, can arrange Trans-Mongolian and Trans-Manchurian trips, with options for homestay accommodation.
● **Russia and Beyond** (☎ 02-9299 5799, toll-free ☎ 1-300-363554, 🖺 02-9262 3438, 🖳 www.russiabeyond.com.au), 191 Clarence St, Sydney, NSW 2000, can arrange Trans-Siberian travel packages starting in Moscow, St Petersburg, Vladivostok or Beijing, including stopovers, transfers, accommodation, sightseeing, flights and visa support.
● **Gateway Travel** (☎ 02-9745 3333, 🖺 02-9745 3237, 🖳 www.russian-gate way.com.au), PO Box 451, 48 The Boulevarde, Strathfield, NSW 2135.

The **China National Tourist Office** (☎ 02-9252 9838, 🖺 02-9252 2728, 🖳 www.cnto.org.au) is at 234 George Street, 11th floor, Sydney, NSW 2000.

Embassies in Australia The **Russian Embassy** (☎ 02-6295 9033, 🖺 02-6295 1847, 🖳 www.australia.mid.ru) is at 78 Canberra Ave, Griffith, ACT 2603. There's also a **consulate** (☎ 02-9326 1866, 🖺 02-9327 5065, 🖳 syd neyrussianconsulate.com) at 7-9 Fullerton St, Woollahra, NSW 2025.

The **Chinese Embassy** (☎ 02-6273 4780, 🖺 02-6273 4878, 🖳 www .au.china-embassy.org) is at 15 Coronation Dr, Yarralumla (Canberra), ACT 2600. There are **consulates** in Sydney (☎ 02-8595 8000, 🖺 02-8595 8021, 🖳 www.sydney.chineseconsulate.org, 39 Dunblane St, Camperdown NSW 2050), Perth (consular office ☎ 08-9222 0333, 🖺 08-9221 6144, 45 Brown St, East Perth, WA 6004), Brisbane (07-3210 6509, 07-3012 8096, : www.brisbane.chi neseconsulate.org; Level 9, 79 Adelaide St, QLD 4000) and Melbourne (☎ 03-9822 0604, 🖺 03-9822 0320, 🖳 www.chinaconsulatemel.org, 75-77 Irving Rd, Toorak, Victoria 3142).

Australia has no consular offices for Mongolia, Belarus or Poland.

From New Zealand
● **Sundowners Adventure Travel** (toll-free ☎ 0800-447 506, 🖺 03-9672 5311, 🖳 www.sundownerstravel.com); these contact details connect to the Sundowners office in Australia (see opposite).
● **Adventure World** (☎ 09-524 5118, 🖺 09-520 6629, 🖳 www.adventure world.co.nz), 101 Great South Rd, Remuera, PO Box 74008, Auckland. New Zealand's biggest adventure-travel wholesaler offers individual and group Trans-Siberian, Trans-Mongolian and Trans-Manchurian journeys.
● **Innovative Travel** (☎ 03-365 3910, toll-free ☎ 0508-100111, 🖺 03-365 5755, 🖳 www.innovative-travel.com), Innovative House, 269 Cashel St, PO Box 21247, Christchurch. Offer tours to Russia but not on the Trans-Siberian.

Embassies in New Zealand The **Russian Embassy** (consular office ☎ 04-476 6742, 🖺 04-476-3843, 🖳 www.rus.co.nz) is at 57 Messines Rd, Karori, Wellington.

The **Chinese Embassy** (☎ 04-472 1382, 🖃 04-499 0419, 🖳 www.chinaem bassy.org.nz) is at 2-6 Glenmore St, Wellington. There is a **consulate** (☎ 09-571 3080, 🖃 09-525 0733, 🖳 www.chinaconsulate.org.nz) at 630 Great South Rd, Greenlane, Auckland.

Belarus, Mongolia and Poland do not have embassies in New Zealand.

MAKING A BOOKING IN SOUTH AFRICA

● **Intourist/Titch Tours** (☎ 021-686 5501, 🖳 www.russiatravel.co.za), 26 Statiion Rd. Rondebosch, Cape Town 7700, will arrange flights, accommodation, train tickets, transfers and visas. They also operate a number of tours.

● **STA Travel** (☎ 0861-781 781, 🖃 011-706 4765, 🖳 www.statravel.co.za) in South Africa has branches in Johannesburg, Pretoria, Bloemfontein, Durban and Cape Town, and can make Trans-Siberian bookings.

Embassies in South Africa The consular office of the **Russian Embassy** (☎ 012-362 7116, 🖃 012-362 7090, 🖳 russianembassy.org.za) is at 316 Brook St, Menle Park, Pretoria 0001. There is also a **consulate** (☎ 021-418 3656, 🖃 021-419 2651, 🖳 rusco@icon.co.za) at Southern Life Centre, 50th Floor, 8 Riebeeck St, Cape Town.

The **Chinese Embassy** (☎ 012-342 4194, 🖃 012-342 4154, 🖳 www.chi nese-embassy.org.za) is at 965 Church St, Arcadia 0083, Pretoria. There are **consulates** at Durban (☎ 031-563 4534, 45 Stirling Crescent, Durban North), Cape Town (☎ 021-674 0579, 25 Rhodes Ave, Newlands) and Johannesburg (☎ 011-685 7540, 25 Cleveland Rd, Sandhurst, Sandton).

MAKING A BOOKING IN JAPAN

● **Euras Tours Inc** (🖳 www.euras.co.jp) is a friendly, efficient agency handling bookings for rail journeys to Europe with a choice of itineraries combining flights, ferries and trains, directly into Russia or via China. They have an office in **Tokyo** (☎ 03-5562 3381, 🖃 03-5562 3380, 1-26-8 Higashi-Azabu, Minato-ku) and in **Osaka** (☎ 06-6531-7416, 🖃 06-6531-7437, 1-11-7 Nishi-Honcho).

● **Intourist Japan** (☎ 03-3238 9118, 🖃 03-3238 9128, 🖳 www.intourist-jpn.co.jp, 2nd floor, Yamazaki Bldg, 4-1-14 Kudan Kita, Chiyoda-ku, Tokyo 102-0073. Can arrange everything you need for a trip on the Trans-Siberian.

The **China National Tourist Office** has branches in Tokyo (☎ 03-3591 8686, 🖃 03-3591 6886, 🖳 www.cnta-osaka.jp; 8th floor, Air China Bldg, 2-5-2 Toranomon, Minato-ku) and in Osaka (☎ 06-635 3280, 🖃 06-635 3281, 4th floor, Ocat Bldg, 1-4-1 Minato-machi, Naniwa-ku).

Embassies in Japan

The consular division of the **Russian Embassy** (☎ 03-3583 4445, 🖃 03-3586 0407, 🖳 www.tokyo.ruembassy.org) is at 1-1 Azabudai, 2-chome, Minato-ku, Tokyo 106-0041. There are **consulates** in Osaka (☎ 06-6848 3451, Toyonaka-shi, Nishi Midorigaoka 1-2-2), Niigata (☎ 025-244 6015, Fai-Biru, 1-20-5 Sasaguchi) and Sapporo (☎ 011-561 3171, 826 Nishi 12-chome, Minami 14-jo, Chuoku).

❏ FERRIES FROM JAPAN

In addition to flights you have several options for travel by ferry from Japan. You may sail to the Russian port of Vladivostok, or to various Chinese ports, all within easy reach of Beijing: Shanghai, Tianjin or Qingdao.

Fushiki (Toyama) to Vladivostok

From mid-May to late December a weekly ferry operates between Fushiki and Vladivostok, a 40- to 45-hour journey. One-way tickets cost from ¥30,800 to ¥97,900 (US$280-890), including meals and the port tax at Vladivostok, with 10% off some fares for students. Agencies where you can purchase tickets include the following:
● **FKK Air Service** (☎ 0766-22 2212, ◫ 22 7456, ▭ http://fkk-air.toyama-net.com/ rus_sennai.html (Japanese), fkk-air@toyama-net.com), Duo Bldg, Shimonoseki-machi 4-56, Takaoka-shi, Toyama 933-0021 FKK also sells flights to Vladivostok.
● **United Orient Shipping & Agency Co** (Tokyo Kyodo Kaiun; ☎ 03-5640 3901, ◫ 03-5640 1633, ▭ www.bisintour.com or www.uniorient.co.jp, ▭ k-yoshida@uniorient.co.jp), Tomare Nihonbashi-Hamacho 9F, 3-2-3 Chuo-ku, Tokyo 103-0007. If writing an email in English put 'Vladivostok Ferry Reservation' as the subject so they know the email is not spam.

For information on the journey **from** Vladivostok, see p321.

Osaka/Kobe to Shanghai

The Chinese-run Japan-China International Ferry Co (JIFCO) runs weekly ferries to Shanghai, with departures from Osaka or Kobe on alternate weeks; and the Shanghai Ferry Co operates a weekly service from Osaka. One-way fares range from ¥20,000 to ¥100,000 including breakfast, with 10% discounts for students. The journey takes approximately 48 hours. From Shanghai it's a 15-hour train journey to Beijing.
● **Japan-China International Ferry Co** has offices in Tokyo (☎ 03-5489 4800, ◫ 03-5489 4788, ▭ www.fune.co.jp/chinjif/index.html, jifcot@dream.com, Daikanyama Pacific Bldg, 10-14 Sarugaku-cho, Shibuya-ku, 150-0033) and Osaka (☎ 06-6536 6541, ◫ 06-6536 6542, Rm 201, Sanai Bldg, 1-8-6 Shinmachi, Nishi-ku, 550-0013).
● **Shanghai Ferry Company** has offices in Osaka (☎ 06-6243 6345, ◫ 06-6243 6308, ▭ www.shanghai-ferry.co.jp, 5F Dai Building, Midosuji, 4-1-2 Minami Kyuhoji-cho, Chuo-ku, 541-0058) and Shanghai (☎ 021-6537 5111, ◫ 021-6537 9111, ▭ zhang yz@suzhaohao.com, 4th floor, The Panorama Shanghai, 53 Huangpu Rd, 20080).

Kobe to Tianjin

China Express Line sails weekly between Kobe and the Chinese port of Tanggu, near Tianjin, a 48-hour trip. One-way fares start at ¥22,000, with a 10% discount for students, and go up to ¥79,000. From Tianjin it's a 1½-2hour train journey to Beijing.
● **China Express Line** (☎ 078-321 5791, ◫ 078-321 5793, ▭ www.celkobe.co.jp/pax/index.html) is at 4-5 Shinkocho, Chuo-ku, Kobe 650-0041. Their Chinese counterpart is the **Tianjin Jinshen Ferry Co** (☎ 022-2420 5777, ◫ 022-2420 5970), 22nd floor, Ocean Shipping Plaza, Hebei District, Tianjin.

Shimonoseki to Qingdao

Japanese-owned Orient Ferry Ltd operates a year-round service between Shimonoseki, on the western tip of Honshu, and Qingdao (3/week), a 27½hour voyage. One-way tickets to Qingdao cost ¥15,000-60,000 with a 20% student discount.
● **Orient Ferry Ltd** (☎ 0832-326615, ◫ 0832-326616, ▭ www.orientferry.co.jp in Japanese), 10-64-1 Higashi-Yamato-cho, Shimonoseki 750-0066).

Tickets for most services can also be bought from branch offices of Japan Travel Bureau and Kintsuri (Kinki Nihon Tourist).

The **Chinese Embassy** (☎ 03-3403 3380, 🖹 03-3403 3345, 💻 www.china-embassy.or.jp/chn) is at 3-4-33 Moto-Azabu, Minato-ku, Tokyo 106-0046.

The **Mongolian Embassy** (☎ 03-3469 2088, 🖹 3469 2216, 💻 www.mnemb.go.jp) is at 21-4 Kamiyama-cho, Shibuya-ku, Tokyo 150-0047.

There is a **Belarus Embassy** (☎ 03-3448 1623, 🖹 03-3584 8064) at Shirogane K House 4-14-12, Shirogane-dai, Minato-ku, Tokyo 108-0072.

MAKING A BOOKING IN CHINA

From Beijing

In the summer trains fill up quickly, so if you plan to spend some time travelling around China, make Beijing your first stop and get your onward travel nailed down. Once you've made your train reservations and paid your deposit, do the rounds of the embassies and collect your visas. You'll need RMB (yuan) as well as crisp US dollar cash, and a stock of passport photos.

Alternatively you may be able to reserve a place on the train while you're in Shanghai (ask at the travel bureau in the Peace Hotel). Shanghai has a Russian consulate (see opposite) but no Mongolian consulate.

● **Monkey Business Infocenter** (☎ 010-6591 6519, 🖹 010-6591 6517, 💻 www.monkeyshrine.com), Room 201, Poachers Inn, 43 Beisanlitun Nan, off Sanlitun Bar St (the entrance is from The Tree Courtyard), open 10:00-18:00 Monday-Saturday.

The 'monkeys' are André and Patrick, Belgian brothers who by now have put thousands of budget travellers on trains across Siberia. They'll organize everything for you, provide visa support for Russia stopovers, even put you on the train. They sell a range of individual packages from Beijing to Moscow (from €485) and a wide range of stopover packages (eg Mongolia, Irkutsk, Lake Baikal and Yekaterinburg). They can even book a journey from Moscow **to** Beijing.

● **CITS Beijing** (☎ 010-6512 0507, 🖹 010-6512 0503, 💻 www.citsbj.com/english), Beijing International Hotel. The cheapest, quickest Trans-Siberian tickets you're likely to find are sold here, although the staff often aren't keen to spend a lot of time answering questions, and availability can be a problem in summer owing to high demand. They're open 08:30-12:00, 13:00-17:00 Monday to Friday.

Embassies in Beijing Of course you'll need a Russian visa, but you're better off getting this at home, because at the time of writing the Russian consulate in Hong Kong was the only Russian consulate in China that would officially accept visa applications from non-residents of China. The Hong Kong consulate was also the only one that would accept faxed or printed copies of invitations or other support documents. An agent can apply to the Hong Kong consulate on your behalf, but there must be a valid Hong Kong entry stamp in your passport.

Other Russian consulates in China, including the one in Beijing, will in fact make exceptions and accept foreigners if they aren't too busy, but only if the applicant has original copies of invitations and other paperwork from Russia.

These are either timely or costly to obtain by post. Transit visas are still possible to obtain from the Beijing consulate, but you'll need your train ticket, and most likely an onward ticket and visas as well. If you want to stop in Mongolia, you must obtain your Russian transit visa there.

For the Trans-Mongolian route, you'll need a Mongolian visa as well, unless you're American or Israeli. If you're continuing through Europe after Moscow you may need a transit visa for Belarus or Ukraine. It's easier to get most visas here than in Moscow, though there is no Ukrainian consulate in Beijing, only in Shanghai.

● **Russia** (consular department ☎ 010-6532 1267, 📄 010-6532 4853, 💻 www .russia.org.cn), 4 Dongzhimen Beizhong Jie, Beijing 100600; open for applications 09:00-12:00 Monday to Friday, but you are strongly advised to get there before 10:30.

There are **Russian consulates** in: Shanghai (☎ 021-6324 8383, 💻 consul @online.sh.cn, 20 Huangpu Lu, Shanghai 200080), Shenyang (☎ 024-2322 3927, 💻 ruscons@pub.sy.ln.cn, Shisan Nanweilu 31, Shenyang 110031) and Hong Kong (☎ 2877 7188, 📄 2877 7166, 💻 cgrushk@hknet.com, 29th floor, Sun Hung Kai Centre, 30 Harbour Rd, Wanchai).

A single-entry tourist or transit visa costs US$50, plus a consular fee which varies with your nationality (currently US$20 for Americans, US$7 for Brits, US$11 for Canadians and US$25 for the EU). The same prices apply to transit visas. In theory double-entry costs US$50 extra, but may not be accepted, or with conditions that you need to break your journey for 30 days before the second entry. Processing normally takes five working days; add US$35 for three working days or US$70 for 24 hours. Prices are displayed in US$ and that's what foreigners are expected to use, but you can pay in RMB at a poor exchange rate. You'll also need one photo and photocopies of the information pages of your passport.

Transit visas from this embassy are normally valid for 10 days from your departure from Beijing, giving you just enough time to get to Moscow and stay a night or two. Check this before you leave the embassy. For a transit visa you will probably have to show onward visa and tickets. If you're stopping off in Russia or spending more than two days in Moscow, you'll need a tourist visa.

Some European nationalities need health insurance to qualify for a Russian visa (see box p21).

● **Mongolia** (☎ 010-6532 3210, 📄 010-6532 5045, 💻 monembbj@public3.bta .net.cn), 2 Xiushui Beijie, Jianguomenwai Dajie, Beijing; the consular section is open for applications 09:00-11:00 Monday to Friday. There is also a Mongolian consular office in Hong Kong, but officially only Hong Kong residents can apply there. In Beijing, a 30-day tourist visa costs US$35 for a five-day service, or add US$25 for an overnight express service. Three-day transit visas cost US$25 for five-day service, or add US$15 for overnight express. You'll need one photo, and for a transit visa you'll need a Russian visa and possibly an onward ticket. Procedures are formal, but staff are helpful.

• **Belarus** (☎ 010-6532 1691, 🖨 010-6532 6417, 🖳 www.belembassy.com), 1 Dong Yi Jie, Ritan Lu, Jianguomenwai, Beijing 100600, open for applications 10:00-12:00 Monday, Wednesday and Friday. For the mandatory 48-hour transit visa you'll need one photo and US$30 for five days' processing; two days' processing costs US$55. The price for Americans is US$120. You may be asked to show your Russian visa.

For information on other embassies in Beijing see p350.

From Hong Kong

Hong Kong can be a good place to arrange a ticket or stopover package on the Trans-Siberian. Most visitors do not require a visa to enter Hong Kong, and this is an easy place to get a visa for onward travel into the rest of China. There's also a **Mongolian embassy** (☎ 3571 8845, 🖳 www.mongolia.com/hk), Rooms 1109-1111 Wayson Comm Building, 28 Connaught Rd West.

Agencies here offer a range of services and booking with them from abroad is usually no problem. Several travel agencies in the Nathan Road area can arrange tickets with a few weeks' notice. Some will sell you a voucher to exchange in Beijing for a reserved ticket. Others sell you an open ticket with a reservation voucher, leaving you to get the ticket endorsed by CITS in Beijing; don't accept an open ticket without a reservation voucher. But to visit any Russian cities apart from Moscow you'll need a tourist visa and therefore visa support.

• **Monkey Business/Moonsky Star** (☎ 2723 1376, 🖨 2723 6653, 🖳 www.mon keyshrine.com, hongkong@monkeyshrine.com), 11th Floor, Flat D, Liberty Mansion, 26E Jordan Rd (entrance at Temple St), Yau Ma Tei, Kowloon; open (by appointment only) 10:00-18:00, Monday to Saturday. This office concentrates on journeys commencing in Hong Kong. If you want to make advance plans, get in touch with their Beijing office (see p352).
• **Global Union Transportation** (☎ 2868 3231, 🖨 2537 2605, 🖳 www.glob al.com.hk), Rm 22-23 New Henry House, 10 Ice House St, Central, has been recommended by several readers for booking Trans-Siberian tickets and helping with Russian visa support.
• **Phoenix Travel** (☎ 2722 7378, 🖨 2369 8884, 🖳 www.statravel.hk, 🖳 info @phoenixtrvl.com), Rm 1404, Austin Tower, 22-6 Austin Ave, Tsim Sha Tsui, Kowloon (Jordan MTR Station Exit D). Agent for STA Travel in Hong Kong.
• **Shoestring Travel** (☎ 2723 2306, 🖨 2721 2085, 🖳 www.shoestringtravel .com.hk, shoetvl@hkstar.com), Flat A, 4th Floor, Alpha House, 27-33 Nathan Rd, Tsim Sha Tsui, Kowloon.

What to take

Woollen underwear is the best safeguard against sudden changes in temperature. High goloshes or 'rubber boots' are desirable, as the unpaved streets of the towns are almost impassable in spring and autumn; in winter felt overshoes or 'arctics' are also necessary. A mosquito-veil is desirable in E. Siberia and Manchuria during the summer. It is desirable to carry a revolver in Manchuria and in trips away from the railway.
Karl Baedeker *Russia with Teheran, Port Arthur and Pekin, 1914*

The best advice today is to travel as light as possible. Some people recommend that you put out everything you think you'll need and then pack only half of it. Remember that unless you're going on an upmarket tour, you'll be carrying your luggage yourself.

CLOTHES

For summer in Moscow and Siberia pack thin clothes, a sweater and a raincoat. In every hotel you will be able to get laundry done, often returned the same day. Take shirts and tops of a quick-drying cotton/polyester mixture if you are going to wash them yourself.

Winter in Russia and northern China is extremely cold, although trains and most buildings are kept well-heated: inside the train you can be quite warm enough in a thin shirt as you watch Arctic scenes pass by your window. When you're outside, however, a thick winter overcoat is an absolute necessity, as well as gloves and a warm hat. It's easy to buy good quality overcoats/jackets in Beijing. If you're travelling in winter and plan to stop off in Siberian cities along the way you might consider taking thermal underwear. Shoes should be strong, light and comfortable; most travellers take sturdy trainers. On the train, Russians discard their shoes and wear flip flops – the type you can wear with socks. This is a good idea and you can buy them at any station or on virtually any street. Russians also wear track-suits throughout the journey, while the Chinese might resort to pyjamas.

If you forget anything, clothes are expensive in Japan, cheap but shoddy in Russia, cheap and fashionable in Hong Kong, and very cheap in China.

LUGGAGE

If you're going on one of the more expensive tours which include baggage handling, take a suitcase. Those on individual itineraries have the choice of rucksack (comfortable to carry for long distances but bulky) or shoulder-bag (not so good for longer walks but more compact than a rucksack). A zip-up holdall with a shoulder strap or a frameless backpack is probably the best bet. It's also useful to take along a small daypack for camera, books etc. Since bedding on the train and in hotels is supplied you don't need to take a sleeping-bag even when

Luggage limits

On my first Trans-Siberian trip from Beijing we had so much luggage that several taxi-drivers refused to take us to the station. Unfortunately all thirteen bags were necessary as we were moving back from Japan. On the train we'd managed to get some of them stowed away in the compartments above the door and under the seats when we were joined by a German woman travelling home after three years in China. Her equally voluminous baggage included two full-size theatrical lanterns which were very fragile. Then the man from Yaroslavl arrived with three trunks. We solved the storage situation by covering the floor between the bottom bunks with luggage and spreading the bedding over it, making a sort of triple bed on which we all lounged comfortably – eating, drinking, reading, playing cards and sleeping for the next six days. Dragging our bags around Moscow, Berlin and Paris was no fun, however. On subsequent journeys I didn't even take a rucksack, only a light 'sausage' bag with a shoulder strap and a small day-pack. Never travel with an ounce more than you absolutely need. Nowadays a 35kg luggage limit in compartments is strictly applied in Beijing but ignored in Moscow.

travelling in winter, although some travellers prefer to carry their own sleeping sheet (a sheet used inside a sleeping bag).

GENERAL ITEMS

Essentials
A **money-belt** is essential to safeguard your documents and cash. Wear it underneath your clothing and don't take it off on the train, as compartments are very occasionally broken into. A good pair of **sunglasses** is necessary in summer as well as in winter, when the sun on the snow is particularly bright. A **water bottle** (two-litre) which can take boiling water is essential as is a **mug** (insulated is best), spoon and knife.

Useful items
The following items are also useful: a few clothes pegs, adhesive tape, ball-point pens, business cards, camera and adequate supplies of film (or memory cards for a digital camera), torch (flashlight), folding umbrella, games (cards, chess – the Russians are very keen chess players – Scrabble etc), lavatory paper, calculator (for exchange rates), notebook or diary, penknife with corkscrew and can-opener (although there's a bottle opener fixed underneath the table in each compartment on the train), photocopies of passport, visa, air tickets, etc (keep them in two separate places), sewing-kit, spare passport photographs for visas, string (to use as a washing-line), the addresses of friends and relatives (don't take your address book in case you lose it), tissues (including the wet variety), universal bathplug (Russian basins usually don't have a plug), washing powder (liquid travel soap is good) and hand soap. Some people take along an electric heating coil for boiling a mug of water when staying in a hotel. A compass is useful when looking at maps and out of the window of the train. Earplugs are useful on the train and in noisy Chinese hotels. Don't forget to take a good book (see p49).

It's also a very good idea to bring things to show people: glossy magazines (the more celebrity pictures the better), photos of your family and friends, your home or somewhere interesting you have been. Everyone will want to look at them, and will often get out photos of their own to show you; the Chinese in particular adore looking at photographs of people. This is a great way to break the ice when you don't speak much of the local language.

Gifts

The Russians are great present givers (see p84), and there's nothing more embarrassing than being entertained in a Russian home when you have nothing to offer in return. Cakes and chocolates can be bought locally, or better, bring things that are harder for Russians to get, such as postcards or souvenirs of your country. Foreign coins and badges are also good, as Russia is full of collectors.

It is essential to ensure that you have things to share while you're on the train, such as chocolate biscuits, sweets or other snacks. If you're trying to impress a Russian with chocolate it has to be good, since Russian chocolate, the Red October brand in particular, can be excellent. Red October's Gold Label bar has been on the market since 1867.

Provisions

Though the menus in Russian restaurant cars are sometimes long, often they'll only have a few items on the list: soup, a meat dish and a few refrigerated salads. Beer, chocolate and biscuits are generally available. There's also a good selection of things to eat available from hawkers on station platforms along the way.

It's wise to buy some provisions before you get on the train, especially if you're going the whole way without a break. Take along fruit, cheese and sausage; you can almost always buy bread, tomatoes, boiled eggs, boiled potatoes, soft drinks and beer on the platform. Vodka is not sold on station platforms, but Russians always know where to find it! If you're sharing a compartment with Russians, they'll probably insist you share their food. To refuse would be rude. You should obviously offer some of your food as well, though often it will not be accepted as they will see you as their guest.

Some travellers bring rucksacks filled with food, though it's more realistic to bring just some biscuits and tea-bags or instant coffee (with whitener and sugar if required); hot water is always available from the samovar in each carriage. Other popular items include drinking chocolate, dried soups, tinned or fresh fruit, fruit-juice powder, peanut butter, Marmite or Vegemite, chocolate,

---

Platform food – see also p123
I rather regretted having taken on so many supplies at Moscow before the journey, when I saw how much was on offer at the informal markets en route. Gastronomic offerings available from the hawkers at the various stations on the route included: fresh fruit and vegetables, bread, savoury pastries, pancakes, ice-cream, potatoes and various other hot dishes. Big city stations, however, often have no hawkers at all.   **Anthony Kay** (UK)

crackers and pot noodles. If you forget to buy provisions at home there are Western-style supermarkets in both Moscow and Beijing where you can stock up with essentials.

Medical supplies

Essential items are: aspirin or paracetamol; lip salve; sunscreen lotion; insect repellent (vital if you're travelling in summer); antiseptic cream and some plasters/bandaids; an anti-AIDS kit containing sterile syringes and swabs for emergency medical treatment. Note that Western brands of tampons and condoms are not always easily available in Russia or China. Bring an extra pair of glasses or contact lenses if you wear them.

You may want to take along something for an upset stomach (Arrêt, for example) but use it only in an emergency, as changes in diet often cause slight diarrhoea which stops of its own accord. Avoid rich food, alcohol and strong coffee to give your stomach time to adjust. Paradoxically, a number of travellers have suggested that it's a good idea to take along laxatives. For vaccination requirements, see pp50-1.

Mobile phones, laptops and music players

Internet cafés are available in every city along the Trans-Siberian route. If you do choose to bring a **laptop**, be aware that in Russia and Mongolia you'll probably be the only person on the train who has one, and it's probably not wise to use it or charge it until you're inside a hotel.

Many travellers bring **mobile phones** on the train, including Russians, and these can be charged using outlets in the carriages. If you have a universal triband phone (most are), it pays to pick up a SIM card from a Russian mobile company if you are spending a lot of time in the country. These are usually available for free; all you pay for are the credits. Your phone will be registered in the city where you buy it, and while local calls there are cheap, roaming charges once you leave that region can get expensive. The cheapest Russian mobile company is Megafon, but they have no coverage between Krasnoyarsk and Khabarovsk. Beeline covers more cities. MTS covers nearly the whole country but is the most expensive.

Portable **CD and tape players** are commonly used, so an iPod doesn't look too conspicuous. Many travellers won't leave home without them.

Photographic equipment

Many Russians and Chinese have digital cameras, so there's no need to feel self-conscious about using one on the train. Batteries can be charged on board

---

Window cleaning
A squeegie, an instrument used by window-cleaners to remove water, can be easily obtained in a small size for car windows. This tool is an invaluable aid for cleaning the train's windows for photography or, for that matter, just for passengers' viewing.   **Robert Bray** (UK)

What not to photograph

Taking pictures from the train used to be forbidden but now it's OK, although it would be wise not to get trigger-happy at aerodromes, military installations or other politically sensitive areas.

Remember that in Russia, as in most other countries, it's considered rude to take pictures of strangers, their children or possessions without asking permission. Often people are keen to have their picture taken but you must always ask. This is particularly the case during political demonstrations or rallies: the updater of an earlier edition of this guide got stoned by a group of pensioners outside the White House for trying to get the next cover for *Time* magazine. Beware!

Refrain from photographing touchy subjects such as drunks, queues and beggars. Photography in churches is normally discouraged, and taking a photo of someone in front of an icon is considered disrespectful. A useful phrase is 'Mozhno vas snimat?' (Можно вас снимать?) meaning simply, 'Can I take a photo of you?' When asking for permission, offer to send them a copy: and keep your word. If travelling in winter always carry your camera inside your pocket or elsewhere near your body, as film gets brittle and batteries get sluggish in the intense cold.

from outlets in the carriages. Every city along the route has digital print shops, and in most internet cafés the staff will burn your photos onto a CD for you if you bring a USB cable. Many travellers on long journeys carry portable hard drives for storing photos.

If you shoot with film, bring more than you think you'll need, as you'll find there's a lot to photograph. Don't forget to bring some faster film for shots from the train (400 ASA). It's wise to carry all your film in a lead-lined pouch (available from camera shops) if you are going to let them go through Russian X-ray machines at airports.

Most major brands of film are available in Russia cities, but slide or high/low ASA film may be difficult to find outside Moscow and St Petersburg. In the large cities in Siberia and China, you can have your film processed in one hour and the quality is acceptable. In Ulan Bator there are plenty of developers with imported machines. Film development is naturally of a high standard in Japan but, unless you request otherwise, prints will be small.

Photography from the train The problem on the train is to find a window that isn't opaque or one that opens. They're usually locked in winter so that no warmth escapes. Opening doors and hanging out will upset the carriage attendants if they catch you; if one carriage's doors are locked try the next, and remember that the kitchen car's doors are always open. Probably the best place for undisturbed photography is right at the end of the train: 'No one seemed to mind if we opened the door in the very last carriage. We got some great shots of the tracks extending for miles behind the train'. (**Elizabeth Hehir**, The Netherlands).

MONEY – see also p76

With certain exceptions, you will have to pay for everything in local currency (roubles in Russia, RMB/yuan in China). Russian hotels must accept roubles, even though some set their rates in dollars or euros.

There are abundant, well-signposted, 24-hour international ATMs in all major cities along the Trans-Siberian, and in Beijing. Most accept Visa, MasterCard and other major cards and give cash advances from your own account, in local currency. This is the most convenient way to get by without carrying a huge stash of cash. Cards are also accepted by many hotels and a growing number of guesthouses, restaurants and shops.

But there are many times when cash is essential, for example when the banks are closed or there are no ATMs, for visa fees at many embassies, and in Mongolian restaurant cars on the Trans-Siberian. It's essential to have a stash of cash, and by far the most useful currency in Russia, Mongolia and China is US dollars. Carry only a small amount in your pocket and the rest safely under your clothing in a moneybelt (worn in bed at night as well as during the day). Keep a second stash somewhere else for emergencies. Although cash may seem more risky than travellers' cheques many Russians carry far larger stashes around with them than you will probably have.

See p76 for tips on what kind of banknotes to bring, and on places in Russia where other currencies are commonly accepted.

In Russia you'll only succeed in cashing travellers' cheques at select banks, and therefore only during weekday banking hours. Few banks are interested in anything but US$ cheques. In China travellers' cheques are accepted at better hotels, though most are very fussy about signatures and will ask for your passport, which can be a problem if you're busy applying for visas. The exchange rate is usually slightly better than for cash, but the difference is too small to matter. You may also be asked to show your original purchase receipts. If your cheques are lost or stolen, you're unlikely to get a swift refund or replacement.

Because of the circulation of outdated and worthless Russian bank notes, and the small difference in the legal and black markets, exchanging money on the street is not recommended.

BACKGROUND READING

A number of excellent books have been written about the Trans-Siberian railway. Several are unfortunately out of print, though they're often available through inter-library loan. The following are well worth reading before you go:

● *Journey Into the Mind's Eye: Fragments of an Autobiography* by Lesley Blanch (1988) is a fascinating book: a witty, semi-autobiographical story of the author's romantic obsession with Russia and the Trans-Siberian Railway.

● *To the Great Ocean* by Harmon Tupper (1965, out of print) gives an entertaining account of Siberia and the building of the railway.

● *Guide to the Great Siberian Railway 1900* by AI Dmitriev-Mamanov (David and Charles 1971 and also out of print) a reprint of the guide originally published by the Tsar's government to publicize their new railway. Highly detailed but interesting to look at.

● *Peking to Paris: A Journey across two Continents* by Luigi Barzini (1973, out of print) tells the story of the Peking to Paris Rally in 1907. The author accompanied the Italian Prince Borghese and his chauffeur in the winning car, a 40hp Itala. Their route took them across Mongolia and Siberia and for some of the journey they actually drove along the railway tracks.

● *The Big Red Train Ride* by Eric Newby. This is a perceptive and entertaining account of the journey he made in the Soviet era, written in Newby's characteristically humorous style.

● *Through Siberia by Accident*, by Dervla Murphy, is a warm and witty account of this very readable adventurer's travels in Siberia and the BAM region in 2003-4.

● *In Siberia* by Colin Thubron is the best modern book for background on Siberia and certainly one you should either read before you go or take with you on the trip. Thubron's excellent earlier travelogue, *Among the Russians*, was written after his travels in Soviet times.

● *The Trans-Siberian Railway: A Traveller's Anthology*, edited by Deborah Manley, is well worth taking on the trip for a greater insight into the railway and the journey, through the eyes of travellers from Annette Meakin to Bob Geldof. Now out of print but available in libraries.

● Paddy Linehan's *Trans-Siberia* (2001) is a warm and easily readable account of a trip made recently – the contemporary flavour shines out a-plenty. You quickly warm to the author's unpretentious style.

● *The Princess of Siberia* (1984) is Christine Sutherland's very readable biography of Princess Maria Volkonskaya, who followed her husband Sergei Volkonsky to Siberia after he'd been exiled for his part in the Decembrists' Uprising. Her house in Irkutsk is now a museum.

● *As Far As My Feet Will Carry Me* (1955, reprinted 2003) is the true story of the escape of German prisoner of war, Clemens Forell, from the Siberian gulag where he was serving a 25-year hard-labour sentence. It's a gripping adventure tale.

● *Stalin's Nose: Travels Around the Bloc* by Rory Maclean (1992). Maclean explores the former Eastern Bloc in a battered Trabant with his elderly aunt Zita and a pig named Winston. He recounts the histories of some of his more notorious relatives, providing in the process a surreal, darkly humorous commentary on communism and its demise.

● *Lenin's Tomb* by David Remnick (1993) is an eyewitness account of the heady Gorbachev era by this articulate former *Washington Post* correspondent.

● *Between the Hammer and the Sickle: Across Russia by Cycle* by Simon Vickers (1994) is a highly entertaining account of an epic bicycle journey from St Petersburg to Vladivostok in 1990. Out of print but available from libraries.

❏ **Internet resources**
Many travel agents have their own websites, some with useful links; see pp24-40.

● **CIS Railway Timetable** – 🖳 www.poezda.net
The best site for timetables throughout Russia. Search by route, station or train number.

● **The Man in Seat Sixty-One...** – 🖳 www.seat61.com
For information on rail travel anywhere in the world this is the best site there is. Helpful for planning rail trips to and from Russia. Includes a comprehensive section on the Trans-Siberian with lots of useful links.

● **Way to Russia** – 🖳 www.waytorussia.net
Perhaps the best commercial site about travelling in Russia. The information is comprehensive and reasonably up to date.

● **Railway Ring** – 🖳 parovoz.com/cgi-bin/rrr.cgi
A venerable site for Russian rail fanatics, with an English version and exhaustive links to other sites on railways in Russia, the Baltic States and elsewhere in the CIS.

● **Library of Congress Russian Info** – 🖳 lcweb2.loc.gov/frd/cs/rutoc.html
In-depth Russian history, culture, religion, politics etc: the on-line version of a book published by the LOC under its Country Studies/Area Handbook Program (1996).

● **Russian Cities On The Web** – 🖳 www.russia.com/cities
A huge series of links to websites about individual cities in Russia.

● **Russian Museums directory** – 🖳 www.russianmuseums.info
A useful site listing all the museums in Russia with a town by town search facility and weblinks to a number of the museums listed.

● **Yahoo! Russia News** – 🖳 fullcoverage.yahoo.com/full_coverage/world/russia/
Round-up of current news stories about Russia, culled from the main news-service websites, both Western and Russian.

● **Russia Today** – 🖳 http://www.einnews.com/russia/
An excellent round-up of Russian news and analysis.

● **Dazhdbog's Grandchildren** – 🖳 www.ibiblio.org/sergei/
Russian folklore, traditions, culture, myths; many useful links too.

● **Oyubilig's Great Mongol Homepage** – 🖳 www.mongols.com
Mongolian traditions, folklore, history and culture.

● **The Buryatia Page** – 🖳 www.buryatmongol.com
A wide-ranging site on Buryat shamanism, folklore, history, and poetry, with very good links.

● **The Red Book** – 🖳 www.eki.ee/books/redbook/foreword.shtml
Scholarly, sobering research (1991) on the ethnic minority communities of the ex-USSR, with lots about 'endangered' Siberian native peoples.

● **Trans-Siberian Web Encyclopedia** – 🖳 www.transsib.ru/Eng/
Lots of Trans-Sib memorabilia, pictures, city notes, chat and links.

● **Famous Russian Paintings** – 🖳 www.museum.ru/museum/paintings
Browse this on-line gallery or go to the (Russian-only) homepage for a general look at what's on offer from Russian Museums.

● **Russian Cuisine** – 🖳 www.ruscuisine.com/
● **Cyrillic–English Language Support** – 🖳 www.russialink.org.uk/keyboard/russi fy.htm Teach your computer to display Russian (Cyrillic) fonts.

● *East of the Sun: The Conquest and Settlement of Siberia* by Benson Bobrick (1993, reprinted 1997). A readable narrative of Russia's conquest of Siberia, a saga which in colour and drama rivals the taming of the American West.

● *Around The Sacred Sea: Mongolia and Lake Baikal on Horseback* by Bartle Bull (1999). In 1993 Bull and two photographers rode north from Mongolia into Siberia and around Lake Baikal, partly a Boys-Own adventure and partly to report on the growing environmental threat to the lake after the collapse of the USSR. The result is an engaging true-life adventure story.

● *The Conquest of a Continent: Siberia and the Russians* by American historian W Bruce Lincoln (1993) captures the ambition and cruelty of Cossacks, fur trappers and military adventurers in the region.

● *A People's Tragedy: The Russian Revolution 1891-1924* by British historian Orlando Figes (1997) is a scholarly work of social and political history that brings this turning point in Russia's history to life. Winner of the 1997 NCR Book Award.

● *A History of Twentieth-Century Russia* by Robert W Service (1997). The eminent British scholar of Russian history looks back at the entire Soviet experiment, from the rise of communism to the collapse of the USSR.

● *Holy Russia* by Fitzroy Maclean (1979, out of print), probably the most articulate and readable of many summaries of European Russian history, includes several topical walking tours.

However well written and accurate they may be, these books are only the impressions of foreign scholars and visitors. You will get a better idea of the Russian mind and soul from Russians' own literature, even the pre-Revolution classics. If you haven't already read them you might try some of the following:

● Dostoyevsky's thought-provoking, atmospheric *Crime and Punishment* (set in the Haymarket in St Petersburg).
● Tolstoy's *War and Peace*.
● Mikhail Bulgakov's surreal masterpiece, *The Master and Margarita*.
● *Dr Zhivago* by Boris Pasternak (whose grave you can visit in Moscow).
● *Memories from the House of the Dead*, a semi-autobiographical account of Dostoyevsky's life as a convict in Omsk.
● *A Day in the Life of Ivan Denisovitch* by Alexander Solzhenitsyn, detailing 24 hours in the life of a Siberian convict.
● *The Gulag Archipelago* by Alexander Solzhenitsyn.

Other guidebooks

● *Siberian BAM Guide: Rail, Rivers and Road* by Athol Yates and Nicholas Zvegintzov (also from Trailblazer) is a comprehensive guide for travellers in north-east Siberia, including the 3400km BAM (Baikal-Amur Mainline) railway in Eastern Siberia and good coverage of the northern end of Lake Baikal and Lena River routes.

● *Trekking in Russia & Central Asia* by Frith Maier (1994) covers parts of Siberia and includes a look at the history of mountaineering in Russia, although it's now a bit out of date.

For further rail travels in Russia there's **Russia by Rail with Belarus and Ukraine** by Athol Yates (Bradt, 1996), covering 50 cities and 300 towns along major rail lines. Trailblazer publishes guides to rail travel in China, Japan, India and several other countries – see p479 for more information.

For information on locomotives, **Soviet Locomotive Types: The Union Legacy** by AJ Heywood and IDC Button is invaluable. It's co-published by Luddenden Press (UK) and Frank Stenvalls (Sweden).

Health precautions and inoculations

No vaccinations are listed as official requirements for Western tourists visiting Russia, China, Mongolia or Japan. Some may be advisable, however, for certain areas (see below). If you plan to spend more than three months in Russia evidence of a recent negative AIDS test is required. Russia now has one of the highest incidences of AIDS infection in the world, 90% of it drug related.

Vaccination services are available in London through **Trailfinders** (☎ 020-7938 3999, 🖳 www.trailfinders.co.uk, 194 Kensington High St) and **British Airways Travel Clinic** (☎ 0845-600 2236, 🖳 www.britishairways.com/travel/healthclinintro, 213 Piccadilly). **Nomad Travellers Store & Medical Centre** (☎ 020-8889 7014, 🖳 www.nomadtravel.co.uk, 3-4 Wellington Terrace, Turnpike Lane) offers travel medical advice, inoculations and supplies.

In the USA the **Center for Disease Control and Prevention** (toll-free ☎ 1-800-311-3435, 🖳 www.cdc.gov) in Atlanta is the best place to contact for worldwide health information.

INOCULATIONS

● **Diphtheria** Ensure that you were given the initial vaccine as a child and a booster within the last 10 years. The World Health Organization recommends a combined diphtheria-tetanus toxoid (DTT) booster.

● **Tetanus** A booster is advisable if you haven't had one in the last 10 years: if you then cut yourself badly in Russia you won't need another.

● **Hepatitis A** Those travelling on tight budgets and eating in cheaper restaurants run a risk of catching infectious hepatitis, a disease of the liver that drains you of energy and can last from three to eight weeks. It's spread by infected water or food, or by utensils handled by infected persons. Gamma globulin antibody injections give immediate but short-term protection (two to six months). A vaccine (trade names Havrix or Avaxim) lasts for twice that time (and up to 10 years if a booster is given within 6 to 12 months).

● **Malaria** If you plan to visit rural areas of south-western China you may be at risk of malaria, a dangerous disease which is on the increase in parts of Asia.

Health and travel insurance
Wherever you're travelling you should have comprehensive health insurance; most travel agents or tour operators can provide this but it is worth checking different providers to get the best level of cover for the cost.

The UK has reciprocal health-care agreements with some countries, including Russia, but not China or Mongolia. Treatment in state hospitals in Russia is free on production of your passport (prescribed medicines need to be paid for); but given the state of most Russian hospitals you're advised to arrange proper health insurance and go to a private clinic if you get ill. EU and EEA citizens will get free or reduced cost treatment (for anything that becomes necessary during a trip) in the Czech Republic, Estonia, Finland, Germany, Hungary, Latvia, Lithuania, and Poland on production of an EHIC. However, visitors are always advised to have comprehensive travel/health insurance as well.

Some nationalities will need **health insurance** before they can get a Russian visa (see box p21).

The malaria parasite (carried by the Anopheles mosquito) is now resistant to chloroquine, so you may need a complex regimen of **anti-malarial tablets** starting before you go and continuing for weeks after you leave the malarial zone.

● **Other** Ensure you've had recent **typhoid**, **polio** and **BCG** (tuberculosis) boosters. Most people are vaccinated against these diseases in childhood. If you're planning to go off the beaten track it's advisable to have a vaccination against **meningococcal meningitis**. Those going on a long trek in Siberia may want to consider a vaccination against **tick-borne encephalitis**. It's also worth considering a pre-exposure rabies vaccination course.

If you're arriving from Africa or South America you may be required to show a **yellow fever** vaccination certificate.

MEDICAL SERVICES

Those travelling with tour groups will be with guides who can contact doctors to sort out medical problems. Serious problems can be expensive, but you'll get the best treatment possible from doctors used to dealing with foreigners. If you're travelling independently and require medical assistance, contact an upmarket hotel for help. In Moscow the best place to go in an emergency is the American Medical Center, in St Petersburg the American Medical Clinic. In St Petersburg, Moscow, Yekaterinburg, Novosibirsk, Irkutsk and Khabarovsk, medical assistance is available at clinics beside MNTK-Iris hotels.

Large hotels in China usually have a doctor in residence. In Beijing, Shanghai and Guangzhou (Canton) there are special hospitals for foreigners. Take supplies of any prescription medicine you may need. Medical facilities in Mongolia are very limited, doctors lack proper training, and some medications are unavailable.

RUSSIA

Facts about the country

GEOGRAPHICAL BACKGROUND

The Russian Federation includes over 75% of the former USSR, but even without the other old Soviet republics it remains the largest country in the world, incorporating 17,175,000 sq km (over 6.5 million square miles) and stretching from well into the Arctic Circle right down to the northern Caucasus in the south, and from the Black Sea in the west to the Bering Strait in the east, only a few kilometres from Alaska. Russia is twice as big as the USA; the UK could fit into this vast country some 69 times.

Climate

Much of the country is situated in far northern latitudes; Moscow is on the same latitude as Edinburgh, St Petersburg almost as far north as Anchorage, Alaska. Winters are bitter: the coldest inhabited place on earth, with temperatures as low as -68°C (-90°F), is Oymyakon, in Yakutia in north-eastern Siberia.

Geography is as much to blame as latitude. Most of Russia is an open plain, stretching across Siberia to the Arctic, and while there is high ground in the south, there are no northern mountains to block the cold Arctic air which blows across this plain. To the west are the Urals, the low range which divides Europe and Asia. The Himalaya and Pamir ranges beyond the southern borders stop warm tropical air from reaching the Siberian and Russian plains. Thus isolated, the plains warm rapidly in summer and become very cold in winter. Olekminsk, also in Yakutia, holds the record for the widest temperature range in the world, from -60°C (-87°F) to a breathtaking summer high of 45°C (113°F). Along the route of the Trans-Siberian, however, summers are rather milder.

Transport and communications

Railways remain the principal means of transport for both passengers and goods, and there are some 87,500km of track in Russia. The heaviest rail traffic in the world is on certain stretches of the Trans-Siberian, with trains passing every few minutes. Although the **road network** is comparatively well-developed (624,000km), few people own cars. As a result some 34% of all passengers, and 45% of all freight, go by rail.

Russia's **rivers** have historically been of vital importance as a communication network. Some of these rivers are huge, and even navigable by ocean-going ships for considerable distances. But ice precludes year-round navigation, and **air travel** is gradually taking over.

Landscape zones: flora and fauna

The main landscape zones of interest to the Trans-Siberian traveller are as follows:

● **European Russia** Flora and fauna west of the Urals are similar to those elsewhere in northern Europe. Trees include oak, elm, hazel, ash, apple, aspen, spruce, lime and maple.

● **Northern Siberia and the Arctic** The *tundra* zone (short grass, mosses and lichens) covers the treeless area in the far north. Soil is poor and much of it permanently frozen. In fact *permafrost* affects over 40% of Russia and extends down into southern Siberia, where it causes building problems for architects and engineers. Wildlife in this desolate northern zone includes reindeer, arctic fox, wolf, lemming and vole. Bird life is richer, with ptarmigan, snow-bunting, Iceland falcon and snow-owl as well as many kinds of migratory water and marsh fowl.

● **The Siberian plain** Much of this area is covered in *taiga*, a Russian word meaning thick forest. To the north the trees are stunted and windblown; in the south they form dark impenetrable forests. More than 30% of all the world's trees grow in this zone. These include larch, pine and silver fir, intermingled with birch, aspen and maple. Willow and poplar line rivers and streams. Much of the taiga forest along the route of the Trans-Siberian has been cleared and replaced with fields of wheat or sunflowers. Parts of this region are affected by permafrost, so that in places rails and roads sink, and houses, trees and telegraph poles often keel over drunkenly. Fauna includes species once common in Europe: bear, badger, wolverine, polecat, ermine, sable, squirrel, weasel, otter, wolf, fox, lynx, beaver, several types of rodent, musk deer, roebuck, reindeer and elk.

● **Eastern Siberia and Trans-Baikal** Much of the flora and fauna of this region is unique including, in Lake Baikal, such rarities as the fresh-water seal. Amongst the ubiquitous larch and pine there grows a type of birch with dark bark, *Betula daurica*. Towards the south and into China and Mongolia, the forests give way to open grassy areas known as *steppes*. The black earth (*chernozem*) of the northern steppes is quite fertile and some areas are under cultivation.

● **The Far Eastern territories: the Amur region** Along the Amur River flora and fauna are similar to those of northern China, and it is here that the rare Amur tiger (see p413) is found. European flora, including trees such as cork, walnut and acacia, make a reappearance in the Far East.

HISTORICAL OUTLINE

The first Russians

Artefacts uncovered in Siberia (see p90) suggest that human history in Russia may stretch back much further than previously believed: 500,000 or more years. In the 13th millennium BC there were Stone Age nomads living beside Lake Baikal.

By the 2nd millennium BC when fairly advanced civilizations had emerged here, European Russia was inhabited by Ural-Altaic and Indo-European peoples. In the 6th century BC the Scythians (whose magnificent goldwork may be seen in the Hermitage) settled in southern Russia near the Black Sea.

Through the early centuries of the 1st millennium AD trade routes developed between Scandinavia, Russia and Byzantium, following the Dnieper River. Trading centres (including Novgorod, Kiev, Smolensk and Chernigov) grew up along the route and by the 6th century AD were populated by Slavic tribes known as *Rus* (hence 'Russian').

The year 830 saw the first of the Varangian (Viking) invasions and in 862 Novgorod fell to the Varangian chief Rurik, Russia's first sovereign.

Vladimir and Christian Russia
The great Tsar Vladimir (978-1015) ruled Russia from Kiev and was responsible for the conversion of the country to Christianity. Until then Slavs worshipped a range of pagan gods, and it is said that in his search for a state religion Vladimir invited bids from Islam, Judaism and Christianity. Islam wasn't compatible with the Slavs' love of alcohol and Judaism didn't make for a unified nation. Vladimir chose Christianity, had himself baptized at Constantinople in 988 AD, and ordered the mass conversion of the Russian people, with whole towns being baptized simultaneously.

The 11th century was marked by continual feuding between his heirs. It was at this time that the northern principalities of Vladimir and Suzdal were founded.

The Mongol invasion and the rise of Muscovy
Between 1220 and 1230 the Golden Horde brought a sudden halt to economic progress in Russia, burning towns and putting the local population to the sword. By 1249 Kiev was under their control and the Russians moved north, establishing a new political centre at Muscovy (Moscow).

All Russian principalities were obliged to pay tribute to the Mongol khans but Muscovy was the first to challenge their authority. Over the next three centuries Moscow gained control of the other Russian principalities and shook off the Mongol yoke.

Ivan the Terrible (1530-84)
When Ivan the Terrible came to the throne he declared himself Tsar of All the Russians and by his successful military campaigns extended the borders of the young country. He was as wild and bloodthirsty as his name suggests: in a fit of anger in 1582 he struck his favourite son with a metal staff, fatally injuring him (a scene conjured up by Ilya Repin in one of his greatest paintings). Ivan was succeeded by his mentally retarded son Fyodor, but real power rested with the regent, Boris Godunov. Godunov himself later became Tsar, ruling from 1598 to 1605.

The early 17th century was marked by dynastic feuding which ended with the election of Michael Romanov (1613-45), first of a line that was to rule until the Revolution in 1917.

An English Tsarina for Ivan Bazilovitch?

In Elizabethan times there were diplomatic and trading links between England and Muscovy whose emissaries and merchants came to London 'dripping pearls and vermin' while Englishmen went to Moscow. Indeed the Tsar had occasion to complain of the behaviour of some of them thereby eliciting a tactful letter from the Queen.

Elizabeth's diplomatic skills brought about a peace between Ivan Bazilovitch and John, King of Sweden, and the former was so grateful to her that 'imagining she might stand his friend in a matter more interesting to his personal happiness, he made humble suit to her majesty to send him a wife out of England'. The Queen chose Anne, sister of the Earl of Huntingdon and of royal Plantagenet blood, but the lady was not willing to risk 'the barbarous laws of Muscovy which allowed the sovereign to put away his czarina as soon as he was tired of her and wanted something new in the conjugal department. The czar was dissatisfied and did not long survive his disappointment', dying in 1584. He is better known to history as Ivan the Terrible and his reputation may well have affected the Queen's thinking when she sorely tried Tsar Boris Godunov's patience with her diplomatic procrastination over his attempts to get an English bride for one of his sons.

(Sources: *The Letters of Queen Elizabeth*, ed. Harrison; *Lives of the Queens of England*, Agnes Strickland; *History of England from the Accession of James II*, Lord Macaulay; Camden's Annals).   **Patricia Major**

Peter the Great and the Westernization of Russia

Peter (1672-1725) well deserves his sobriquet, 'the Great', for it was his policy of Westernization that helped Russia emerge from centuries of isolation and backwardness into the 18th century. He founded St Petersburg in 1703 as a 'window open on the West' and made it his capital in 1712. During his reign there were wars with Sweden and Turkey. Territorial gains included the Baltic provinces and the southern and western shores of the Caspian Sea.

Peter's extravagant building programme in St Petersburg continued under Catherine the Great (1762-96). While her generals were taking the Black Sea steppes, the Ukraine and parts of Poland for Russia, Catherine conducted extensive campaigns of a more romantic nature with a series of favourites in her elegant capital.

Alexander I and the Napoleonic Wars

In 19th century Russia the political pendulum swung back and forth between conservatism and enlightenment. The mad Tsar Paul I came to the throne in 1796, only to be murdered five years later. He was succeeded by his son Alexander I (1801-25) who was said to have had a hand in the sudden demise of his father. Alexander abolished the secret police, lifted the laws of censorship and would have freed the serfs had the aristocracy not objected so strongly to the idea. In 1812 Napoleon invaded Russia, and Moscow was burnt to the ground (by its inhabitants, not by the French) before he was pushed back over the border.

RUSSIA

Growing unrest among the peasants

Nicholas I's reign began with the first Russian Revolution, the Decembrists' uprising (see p98), and ended, after he had reversed most of Alexander's enlightened policies, with the Crimean War against the English and French in 1853-6. Nicholas was succeeded by Alexander II (1855-81) who was known as the Tsar Liberator, for it was he who finally freed the serfs. His reward was his assassination by a student in St Petersburg in 1881. He was succeeded by the strong Alexander III, during whose reign work began on the Trans-Siberian Railway.

Nicholas II: last of the Tsars

The dice were heavily loaded against the unfortunate Nicholas. He inherited a vast empire and a restless population that was beginning to discover its own power. In 1905 his army and navy suffered a humiliating defeat at the hands of the Japanese. Just when his country needed him most, as strikes and riots swept through the cities in the first few years of the 20th century, Nicholas's attention was drawn into his own family crisis. It was discovered that Alexis, heir to the throne, was suffering from haemophilia. The Siberian monk, Rasputin, ingratiated his way into the court circle through his ability to exert a calming influence on the Tsarevich. His influence over other members of the royal family, including the Tsar, was not so beneficial.

October 1917: the Russian Revolution

After riots in 1905, Nicholas agreed to allow the formation of a national parliament (Duma), though its elected members had no real power. Reforms came too slowly for the people and morale fell further when, during the First World War, Russia suffered heavy losses.

By March 1917 the Tsar had lost control and was forced to abdicate in favour of a provisional government led by Alexander Kerensky. But the Revolution that abruptly changed the course of Russian history took place in October of that year, when the reins of government were seized by Lenin and his Bolshevik Party. The Tsar and his family were taken to Siberia where they were murdered (see p228). Civil war raged across the country and it was not until 1920 that the Bolsheviks brought the lands of Russia under their control, forming the Union of Soviet Socialist Republics (USSR).

The Stalin era

After Lenin's death in 1924 control passed to Stalin and it was under his leadership that the USSR was transformed from a backward agricultural country into an industrial world power. The cost to the people was tremendous and most of those unwilling to swim with the current were jailed for their 'political' crimes. During the Great Terror in the 1930s, millions were sentenced to work camps, which provided much of the labour for ambitious building projects.

During the Second World War the USSR played a vital part in the defeat of the Nazis and extended its influence to the East European countries that took on Communist governments after the war.

Khrushchev, Brezhnev, Andropov and Chernenko

After Stalin died in 1953 Nikita Khrushchev became Party Secretary and attempted to ease the strict regulations which governed Soviet society. In 1962 his installation of missiles in Cuba almost led to war with the USA.

Khrushchev was forced to resign in 1964, blamed for the failure of the country's economy and for his clumsy foreign policy. He was replaced by Brezhnev who continued the USSR's policy of adopting friendly 'buffer' states along the Iron Curtain. He ordered the invasion of Afghanistan in 1979 'at the invitation of the leaders of the country'.

When Leonid Brezhnev died in 1982, he was replaced by the former head of the KGB, Yuri Andropov. He died in 1984 and was succeeded by the elderly Konstantin Chernenko, who managed a mere 13 months in office before becoming the chief participant in yet another state funeral.

Gorbachev and the end of the Cold War

Mikhail Gorbachev, the youngest Soviet premier since Stalin, was elected in 1985 and quickly initiated a process of change known by the terms *glasnost* (openness) and *perestroika* (restructuring). He is credited in the West with bringing about the end of the Cold War (he received the Nobel Prize in 1990) but it would be misguided to think of him as sole architect of the changes that took place in the USSR: it was widely acknowledged before he came to power that things had gone seriously wrong.

Gorbachev launched a series of bold reforms: Soviet troops were pulled out of Afghanistan, Eastern Europe and Mongolia, political dissidents were freed, laws on religion relaxed and press censorship lifted. These changes displeased many of the Soviet 'old guard,' and on 19 August 1991, a group of senior military and political figures staged a coup. Gorbachev was isolated at his Crimean villa and Vice-President Gennadi Yanayev took over, declaring a state of emergency. Other politicians, including the President of the Russian Republic, Boris Yeltsin, denounced the coup and rallied popular support. There were general strikes and, after a very limited skirmish in Moscow (three casualties), the coup committee was put to flight.

The collapse of the USSR

Because most levels of the Communist Party had been compromised in the failed coup attempt, it was soon seen as corrupt and ineffectual. Gorbachev resigned his position as Chairman in late August and the Party was abolished five days later.

The Party's collapse heralded the demise of the republic it had created, and Gorbachev began a desperate struggle to stop this happening. His reforms, however, had already sparked nationalist uprisings in the Baltic republics, Armenia and Azerbaijan. Despite his suggestions for loose 'federations' of Russian states, by the end of 1991 the USSR had split into 15 independent republics. Having lost almost all his support, Gorbachev resigned and was relieved by Yeltsin.

Yeltsin vs the Congress of Deputies

Yeltsin's plans for economic reform were thwarted at every turn by the Congress of People's Deputies (parliament). Members of Congress, elected before the collapse of communism, were well aware that by voting for reforms they were, in effect, removing themselves from office. In the Western press this struggle was described as the fight between reformists (Yeltsin and his followers) and hardliners (Vice President Alexander Rutskoi, Congress Speaker Ruslan Khasbulatov and the rest of Congress). Yeltsin's hard-won referendum in April 1993 gave him a majority of 58% but not a mandate to overrule parliament.

On 22 September 1993 Yeltsin suddenly dissolved parliament and declared presidential rule (some have suggested that this swift action was to avert another coup attempt). The Congress denounced his action, stripped him of power and swore in Rutskoi as President. The Constitutional Court ruled that, having acted illegally, Yeltsin could now be impeached. Khasbulatov accused him of effecting a 'state coup' and appealed for a national strike.

The deciding factor in the confrontation between parliament and president was the loyalty of the military. Rutskoi, an Afghan war veteran with a keen military following, ordered troops to march on Moscow. They never did, but some 5000 supporters responded by surrounding the White House. Inside, the Congress voted to impeach Yeltsin, who retaliated by severing their telephone lines. The White House vigil turned into a siege; electricity lines were cut and the building surrounded by troops faithful to Yeltsin.

On 3 October a crowd of 10,000 communist supporters converged on the White House where Rutskoi exhorted the people to seize the Kremlin and other strategic locations around the city. All through the night there were confrontations as rioters attacked the mayor's office, the Tass news service building and the main TV station. At dawn on 4 October Yeltsin's troops stormed the White House. Fighting went on for most of the day but by evening the building, charred and battered, was taken. By the end of the week, when order had been restored, 171 people had been killed.

Zhirinovsky and Chechnya

State elections in December 1993 supported Yeltsin's draft constitution, which outlined Russia's new democratic architecture. Although the immediate threat was seen to be rejection of the constitution (Yeltsin warned that this might lead to civil war), the election revealed a new problem in the form of the Liberal Democrat Party. Its leader, Vladimir Zhirinovsky, espoused some extremely sinister policies. Particularly worrying were his comments about reuniting the former USSR, his racist jibes and his aim of re-establishing a Russian empire reaching 'from Murmansk to Madras'.

Yeltsin, in a move to demonstrate his leadership, warn other republics against separatism and regain control over the region's oil industry, ordered Russian troops into the breakaway Russian republic of Chechnya in December 1994. This attempt at a military solution to a political problem was to saddle Russia with its deadliest domestic issue for decades. By the time a truce was signed in May 1996 over 80,000 Russian and Chechen soldiers and civilians had died. The refusal to countenance Chechen demands for independence has made the issue all but intractable. The truce, and a subsequent ceasefire and peace accord have all failed to quench the violence.

1996 presidential elections

Zhirinovsky's star had fallen by the start of the 1996 election campaign: it appeared that the winner would be communist leader Gennadi Zyuganov, but Yeltsin showed his formidable political skills, winning the first round with a fistful of electoral bribes, a promise of strict media control and the backing of the nation's richest entrepreneurs. Interestingly, Gorbachev polled less than 3%. The popular General Alexander Lebed posed a last-minute threat but finally supported Yeltsin in return for his appointment as chairman of the powerful National Security Council, tipping the scales in Yeltsin's favour.

Immediately after his victory Yeltsin disappeared from public view and it soon became obvious that the campaign had taken a serious toll on the hard-drinking president. For nearly four months Russia was virtually leaderless, and power plays were the only decisions being made in the Kremlin. In early 1997 Yeltsin was back and by the end of the year some progress had been made. Inflation was under control and the rouble had been stabilized. Unfortunately the Asian economic crisis of 1998 spoiled Russia's success, and a huge drop in oil exports was followed by the withdrawal of many foreign investors.

Putin's rise to the presidency

In August 1999 Yeltsin fired his fourth prime minister in 18 months and installed Vladimir Putin, an ex-KGB officer, in the post. On New Year's Eve, to everyone's surprise, Yeltsin resigned and handed presidential power to Putin. Three months later Putin won the presidential election with just 52.5% of the vote, pledging to clean up Russia and transform it into a 'rich, strong and civilized country'.

Continuing violence in Chechnya began spilling beyond its borders. After a series of deadly apartment-block bombings in Moscow and other Russian cities were blamed on Chechen terrorists, Putin sent Russian troops back into the province in September 1999. An estimated 200,000 civilians fled into neighbouring republics, and by early 2000 much of Grozny, the Chechen capital, had been razed to the ground. In October 2002 Chechen rebels seized a Moscow theatre, holding 800 people hostage until Russian troops stormed the building, killing most of the rebels and some 180 hostages. When two suicide bombers blew themselves up at a Moscow rock concert in July 2003, officials blamed the Chechens. These and the September 11 attacks in the USA have given free rein to the president's hard-line approach in Chechnya, though no solution is in sight.

Putin's past career as a KGB spy has clearly left him with authoritarian tendencies, and he has shown himself to be no friend of free speech. Email and internet usage is monitored, and reporters and press barons have been hounded. Most worryingly, the Duma approved a law giving the president the right to declare a state of emergency and close down political parties whenever he sees fit to do so.

RUSSIA

On the positive side, Putin has overhauled the tax system, making it simpler to operate and harder to evade, and seems committed to protecting property rights and a liberalized economy. But many in Russia and the West worry that he may take things too far and send Russia spiralling back into a police state, particularly after former FSB (federal security service) agent and Kremlin critic Alexander Litvinenko died an excruciating death from radiation poisoning in a London hospital in November 2006, in a suspected KGB hit job.

In an interview during the G8 summit in 2007, Putin said, 'I'm a pure and absolute democrat. It's a tragedy that I'm the only one. Since Mahatma Gandhi there has been no one' (*The Times*, 4th June 2007).

New wealth and old troubles

In recent years Western commentators have stepped up their public criticism of Putin, seizing on his strong-armed moves to consolidate control of television news coverage. The arrest of oil tycoon Mikhail Khodorkovsky at gunpoint on a Siberian airport runway in October 2003 gave the Kremlin's opponents further fuel. The Western press painted Khodorkovsky as a champion of liberal democracy who was made to suffer for supporting political groups opposed to the Kremlin. His detractors said the oligarch should answer for irregularities during the privatization of his company, Yukos, in the 1990s. In May 2005 he was sentenced to nine years in prison for tax evasion.

The Kremlin's handling of terrorist attacks and the ongoing conflict in Chechnya have also been criticized. In September 2004 Chechen terrorists seized a school in the Russian town of Beslan in North Ossetia. Shooting broke out three days later between the terrorists and Russian troops; according to official data 344 people were killed, 186 of them children, with hundreds more wounded.

Rising oil prices have significantly boosted Russia's economic fortunes. Russia is the world's leading producer of natural gas, boasting 30 percent of the world's known reserves and giving the former superpower renewed clout on the international scene as oil supplies dwindle. Petroleum accounts for 40 percent of Russian GDP and more than 60 percent of its export revenues. Putin has played a game of high-stakes brinksmanship on the world energy market and hasn't always emerged the winner.

On 1 January 2006, the very day Russia took over chairmanship of the G8 group of industrialized nations, Russia cut its gas exports to Ukraine after that country failed to reach an agreement with Gazprom over a proposed rate hike. The cut-off negatively affected gas flow in Eastern and Western European countries as well, and tarnished Russia's image as a reliable energy and trade partner.

Russia has also shown signs of trying to drive out international influence inside its borders. A law passed in January 2006 made it more difficult for foreign non-governmental organizations to operate in the country. The Kremlin has said it suspects some NGOs may harbour spies. And in December 2006, bowing to pressure from the Russian government, Shell Oil offered to hand over its controlling interest in the US$20 billion Sakhalin-2 energy project to state-owned Gazprom. This was widely viewed in the West as a strong-armed tactic reminiscent of Russia's days as a state-controlled economy.

Meanwhile, the war in Chechnya continues. Russian control of the breakaway Muslim province seemingly relies on large-scale detainment and torture. The war and the threat of Chechen terrorism have cost the Russian state greatly and are largely responsible for the clampdown on internal migration that affects Russians and tourists alike; travellers now must register with the authorities within three days of arrival in each town (see p21).

The *Economist* rates Russia as a 'hybrid regime' ruled by 'some form of democratic government.' If you ask Russians, most will tell you that Putin is a 'good leader' and that the country needs a strong hand. If an authoritarian approach is needed to bring order and keep Russia together, they say with a shrug, then so be it.

ECONOMY

Russia has vast natural resources and in this sense is an extremely rich country. It has the world's largest reserves of natural gas as well as deposits of oil, coal, iron ore, manganese, asbestos, lead, gold, silver and copper that will continue to be extracted long after most other countries have exhausted their supplies. Russia's forested regions cover an area almost four times the size of the Amazon basin. Yet owing to gross economic mismanagement under communism and continuing corruption since the privatization of state industries, the country is experiencing severe financial hardship and has been receiving Western aid since 1990.

Privatization

Mass privatization started in the early 1990s. In an attempt to win public approval for the process, in October 1992 every citizen received vouchers worth 10,000 roubles (about US$60 at that time), which could be sold for cash or exchanged for shares in the growing number of private companies. Although the idea of buying and selling stocks caught on, confusion remained over how exactly the market works. Western economic advisers were often asked such questions as 'If I own part of the company, why can't I take the computer home?'

Over 150,000 organizations were privatized but it is now obvious that privatization did nothing to benefit the average Russian. The country's raw materials and viable industries were mostly sold at closed auctions to officially preferred banks and tycoons, with workers left to purchase economically unviable factories and collective farms. Consequently, a relatively small number of well-connected business people pocketed most of Russia's new wealth while millions of workers were lumbered with worthless investments.

Hyperinflation in the 1990s

When once-regulated commodities markets were freed in January 1992, prices immediately soared by 300-400%. Inflation had already been stoked by a 1990 law allowing possession of hard currency, which led to a rush for dollars. Another factor fuelling inflation was an old agreement allowing former

Communist Bloc countries to pay off some debts to Russia in roubles. These countries simply printed up rouble notes, further aggravating Russia's problems. In late 1993 inflation was running at around 25% per month. By the end of 1996 it had dropped to 2% but in 1997 the rouble started to dive again, and Russians sought desperately to change rouble savings into dollars before they became worthless. Foreign investment started to dry up.

In August 1998 Yeltsin took the major decision to devalue the currency: three zeros were knocked off to make the exchange rate six roubles to the dollar; new banknotes were printed and strict new rules governed access to foreign currency.

After dropping further to about 50 roubles to the dollar, the rate has more or less stabilized, wavering around 26 roubles to the dollar in 2007, with inflation running at around 10-13%.

Economic future

Russia is heavily dependent on its energy resources, mainly oil and gas, which account for about 40% of exports, and the economy is very sensitive to global energy prices. High world oil prices in 1999-2000 gave the country a revenue windfall, a jump of 8% in Gross Domestic Product (GDP) and a big boost in its recovery from the 1998 crisis, although growth has been slower since then and the outlook for the future is cloudy. In June 2002 the G8 group of industrialized countries agreed to explore the cancellation of some of Russia's Soviet-era debts.

Putin has brought in a much-needed reform of the tax system. In 1996 only 16% of Russian enterprises paid their taxes in full and on time and only 14 regions out of Russia's 75 paid their tax bills in full. For most people there's now a flat tax rate of 13% with 1% set aside for welfare; corporate taxes have been simplified, too, the idea being that if taxes are low and fair, people will pay. It is estimated that over the last decade taxes amounting to US$150 billion have not been collected.

The country's enormous backlog of wages is gradually being addressed and government coffers are slowly filling. In 2002 Russia had its first surplus budget since the fall of the Soviet Union, yet investment from abroad hasn't materialized to the extent many had hoped. In summer 2005, Putin tried to woo Rupert Murdoch and other tycoons in a private meeting. They complained that Russia's murky legal system and the presence of mafia-like power cliques make its environment too uncertain.

In many respects, things seem to be looking up for Russia. But ask anyone in the street and you'll find that for average people, real life is as tough as ever.

THE PEOPLE

Russia is the sixth most populous nation in the world with an estimated 143.1 million people (about half the population of the former USSR), but it is also one of only a few countries in the world with a declining population: Russia's is dropping by some two-thirds of a million per year, with drug use, alcoholism, sexually transmitted diseases and deteriorating medical care among suggested causes. Average life expectancy is 72 years for Russian women and just 59 years for men.

A high proportion of Russia's people (82%) are ethnic Russians. The rest belong to nearly 100 ethnic minorities, the most numerous being Tatars (4%) and Ukrainians (3%). In the former USSR it was never wise to refer to people as 'Russian' because of the many other republics they might have come from. With the establishment of independence for many of these states you must be even more careful: Kazakhs or Ukrainians, for example, will not appreciate being called Russians.

Russia is divided into *oblasts* (the basic administrative unit), *krays* (smaller territories) and *autonomous republics* (special territories containing ethnic minority groups such as the Buryats in Siberia). Siberia is part of the Russian Federation and exists only as a geographical, not a political, unit.

GOVERNMENT

Russia moved briskly down the political path from autocracy to 'socialist state', with a period of a few months in 1917 when it was a republic. From November 1917 until August 1991 the country was in the hands of the Communist Party, and until September 1993 it was run by the Congress of People's Deputies. This 1068-seat forum was elected from throughout the USSR. At its head sat the Supreme Soviet, the legislative body, elected from Congress. Since only Party members could stand for election in Congress, only Party members could ever run the country.

The approval of a new Russian Constitution in December 1993 means that the country is now governed by a European-style two-tier parliament very similar to that of France. The head of state is the Russian president, currently Vladimir Putin.

Despite the theory, Russia is far from democratic. The power of the country is vested in a few hundred chief executives of huge corporations who picked up enormous wealth through the corrupt privatization of state enterprises. These so-called 'oligarchs' now monopolize the media, gas and oil, military production and banking sectors, in effect controlling the entire Russian state. Seven of these tycoons bankrolled the 1996 Yeltsin re-election and were rewarded with powerful government positions. With these monopolistic and in many cases criminal power merchants securely lodged in the Kremlin, true democracy is a long way off. Under Putin's autocratic control the situation has not changed.

EDUCATION AND SOCIAL WELFARE

Education and health care are provided free for the entire population but standards for both are falling. School is compulsory between the ages of seven and seventeen, with the result that Russia has a literacy rate of 98%. Although funding for research is currently at an all-time low, until a few years ago the country ploughed some 5% of national income directly into scientific research in its 900 universities and institutes. Russia's present inability to maintain its scientists has led to a severe brain drain; certain states in the Middle East are very keen for Russian scientists to help them with their nuclear programmes.

The national health care programme is likewise suffering through lack of funds. Russia has produced some of the world's leading surgeons, yet recent outbreaks of diseases extinct in the developed world have demonstrated that health services here were never comprehensive. The most publicized epidemic in the last few years has been diphtheria, with the death of hundreds of Russians who should have been inoculated at birth.

On his re-election in 1996 Yeltsin promised a high priority for social reform and for raising the living standards of ordinary Russians. Market reforms had seen real incomes fall by 40% between 1991 and 1996, boosted unemployment to 6.6 million and driven a quarter of Russians below the poverty line (US$100 a month). Salaries have risen, but unemployment is sharply up and the fraction of Russians living below the poverty line has continued to rise. The country's external debt, US$38 million in 1987 under the communists, is now US$170 billion.

Recent government programmes aim to stabilize living standards, gradually reduce poverty and mass unemployment, and create conditions for real growth in income. To even the most optimistic Russian, these programmes have virtually no chance of success.

RELIGION

Russia was a pagan nation until 988 when Tsar Vladimir ordered a mass conversion to Christianity. The state religion adopted was that of the Greek Orthodox Eastern Church (Russian Orthodox) rather than Roman Catholicism. After the Revolution religion was suppressed until the late 1930s when Stalin, recognizing the importance of the Church's patriotism in time of war, restored Orthodoxy to respectability. This policy was reversed after the war and many of the country's churches, synagogues and mosques were closed down. Labour camps were filled with religious dissidents, particularly under Khrushchev.

Gorbachev's attitude towards religion was more relaxed and the 1990 Freedom of Conscience law took religion off the blacklist. In 1991 Yeltsin even legalized Christmas: Russian Christmas Day, celebrated on 7 January, is now an official public holiday again. Numerous churches have been restored to cater for the country's estimated 50 million Orthodox believers. In 1997 the Cathedral of Christ the Saviour, demolished by Stalin to make way for a public swimming-pool, was rebuilt in Moscow (see p163). The new cathedral was the setting for a magnificent service on 20 August 2000 in which Tsar Nicholas II and his family, the arch-victims of communism and the Revolution, were made saints in an elaborate canonization ceremony.

As well as Russian Orthodox Christians there are also about 1.4 million Roman Catholics. Numbers of Christian sects are growing. Sects as diverse as the so-called 'Old Believers' (who split from the Orthodox church in the 17th century), Scientology and Jehovah's Witnesses are looking for converts here.

This has worried some Russians, and on 14 June 1993 the Supreme Soviet passed an amendment to the Freedom of Conscience law banning foreign organizations from recruiting by 'independent' religious activities without permission.

Although the number of Muslims has fallen with the independence of the Central Asian Republics, there are still about 11 million in Russia.

Russian Jews, historically subject to the most cruel discrimination, have been less trusting of the greater religious freedoms. Their position has been made even less comfortable by the recent growth of Russian neo-Nazi groups and by the canonization of the last tsar, a confirmed anti-Semite. In 1990 more than 200,000 Jews moved to Israel, pouring in at a rate of up to 3000 per day. By 1998 over half a million had left, though there are still large Jewish communities in Moscow and St Petersburg.

In Buryatia, the centre of Russian Buddhism, many monasteries have reopened. Since all are a long way off the tourist track, they have not been kept in good repair as museums, unlike churches in European Russia.

Religious freedoms have also brought a growth in animism and Shamanism, particularly in Siberia.

Practical information for the visitor

R U S S I A

ESSENTIAL DOCUMENTS

(Also see Part 1: Planning Your Trip.) One 19th-century English traveller who left his passport and tickets behind in London still managed to travel across Siberia carrying no other document than a pass to the Reading Room at the British Library. Entry requirements for foreigners are somewhat stricter nowadays.

The essential documents are your passport, a Russian visa (a page-sized sticker in your passport) and, if appropriate, a visa for the countries you'll be entering after Russia. If you are travelling with an organization which has issued you with vouchers to exchange for accommodation or train tickets, don't forget these. **Always carry your passport on you in Russia**: if the police stop you and you don't have it on you, you'll be fined.

It's worth bringing photocopies of your Russian visa and the information pages from your passport, which are useful when applying for visas. Note that **all visas must be registered within three business days of your arrival in each Russian city**. Failure to do this will make leaving the country difficult without payment of a fine (as high as US$500 but usually less) and will make extending a visa almost impossible.

If you want to rent a self-drive car in Russia you'll need an international driving licence (available from your country's automobile club). International student cards are useful for discounts at major museums in Moscow and St Petersburg.

If you're arriving from Africa or South America you may be required to show a yellow fever vaccination certificate.

CROSSING THE BORDER

Customs allowances: entering or leaving the country

You should not have any problem bringing into Russia any items for personal use or consumption, including modest amounts of spirits or wine. Note that you need a special permit to export 'cultural treasures', a term used to include almost anything that looks old or valuable. Paintings, gold and silver items made before 1968, military medals and coins attract the attention of customs officials and may be confiscated or charged at 100% or more duty if you do not have a permit from the Ministry of Culture. You're currently allowed to import currency up to the value of US$10,000 without declaring it at customs.

Customs declaration form

In the past, at a Russian border you used to be given a Customs Declaration Form (*tamozhennaya deklaratsiya*, таможенная декларация) on which you had to declare all the money and luggage you were carrying. Each time you cashed a travellers' cheque the form was stamped and then checked against your remaining money when you left to ensure you'd been changing money officially. The system was subject to abuse by crooked officials looking for a bribes and now seems to have been abandoned. If, however, you are given such a form on entering the country you should follow its instructions and list your money and valuables on it and also get it stamped on entry. You should then keep this form to be checked when you leave the country.

China no longer requires visitors to fill in a separate customs form; Mongolia still does but may soon follow China's example.

Border-crossing procedure

Border-crossing procedures in the train may take anywhere from three to seven hours. The first step is for immigration and customs officers of the country you are leaving to check passports and visas and collect customs forms. They may disappear with your passport for half an hour or so, and the train might even move during this time; don't worry, but of course don't forget to get it back! The compartments are then searched by border guards looking for stowaways. On the other side of the border the entire procedure is repeated.

Yes sir, whatever you say, sir
It's never a good idea to act smart in front of border guards, but this is perhaps nowhere more true than in Russia. A disturbing study reported by the Russian ITAR-TASS news service states that about 60% of Russia's border guards are so unstable they shouldn't be allowed to carry guns. The study, released two days after a guard in eastern Siberia killed five of his colleagues on a shooting rampage, was based on tests conducted by doctors, psychologists and lawyers following a series of similar shootouts by border guards over the previous two years.

As rails in Russia and Mongolia are of a wider gauge (ie wider apart) than those in China and most of Europe, bogies have to be changed at the borders. The carriages are lifted individually and the bogies rolled out and replaced. If you do not want to stay on the train during this time, you can wait at the border station. If you do get off, carriage attendants won't normally let you get back on before the official boarding time, which is when the train returns to the station to pick up the passengers. Don't leave valuables behind.

Bear in mind that during the entire border crossing procedure the train's lavatories remain locked. This is not purely for security reasons since changing the bogies requires workers to operate beneath the train.

WHERE TO STAY

There's now a wide range of places to stay in Russia: everything from B&Bs (homestays) to luxurious hotels of an international standard. Generally, though, Russian hotels are of gargantuan proportions and about as architecturally interesting as a multi-storey car park. This having been said, some old hotels in Moscow and St Petersburg have been restored to a very high standard.

The old two-tier hotel pricing system for Russians and foreigners, thankfully, is gone. But it's unlikely you'll be offered the most affordable room without asking. Many hotels will let you occupy one bed in a twin-bedded room, paying half the room price but getting the whole room to yourself. This is usually cheaper than a single room, so it's worth asking if you're on a budget.

Types of accommodation

Top hotels Many are owned by large Western chains such as Marriott and Radisson. While they look glitzy like international hotels everywhere, the service still has a touch of Soviet reticence about it. Their restaurants are normally excellent, they have banking facilities, room service and shops, and their staff are motivated. These hotels are mostly found in Moscow and St Petersburg and prices are what you would expect in the West – US$200-500/£115-285 /€165-415 per night.

Standard hotels These are mostly solid old Soviet-era hotels. They have all the tourist facilities of restaurants, banks and shops. Their rooms were once good but lack of maintenance and interest has resulted in some decay. In Moscow and St Petersburg standard hotel rooms cost US$50-200/£25-115 /€40-165 and in other cities US$25-60/£15-35 /€20-50.

Basic hotels These places are usually clean if basically equipped. They normally have a restaurant but no shops, foreign exchange or room service. Rooms are simple with a TV and fridge and either an attached or shared bathroom. If you don't look too closely, the rooms are generally adequate. The best rooms are referred to as *lyuks* ('luxury') and most hotels have at least one such room. This is a relative term and just means that it's the best of all the rooms in that hotel. Basic hotel rooms range from US$15-50/£10-30 /€12-40.

Train station rooms Most train stations have a rest room (*komnata otdykha* Комната отдыха) where you can stay overnight. Sometimes you'll be asked to show a ticket for a train departing the next day. These rooms are very basic with singles, doubles and dormitories available and the bathrooms are shared. Dorm beds generally cost US$20/£10 /€15.

Youth hostels A few cities in Russia, including Moscow, St Petersburg and Irkutsk, have youth hostels. Standards are about what you would expect in the West. Dormitory beds cost about US$20-30/£10-17 /€15-25 a night including basic breakfast. Several places in St Petersburg and Moscow belong to Hostelling International, so it could be worthwhile to invest in an HI card for the discount. Information on youth hostels can be obtained from the Russian Youth Hostel Association (🖥 www.hostelling-russia.ru) or Hostels.com (🖥 www.hostels.com/ru.html).

Holiday homes (*Dom otdykha* Дом отдыха) In the Soviet era these were holiday destinations for city dwellers. They were like country hotels and offered meals and some organized activities. Today the ones that still operate are mostly run-down and often do not even have a restaurant. A few are excellent and remain the holiday choice of the country's élite.

Sanatoria (*Sanatory* Санаторий) These are similar to holiday homes with the addition of a sauna, therapeutic services and mud or spring pools. You do not have to be sick to stay at one and many locals visit them once a year in the belief that this will keep them healthy for another year.

Homestays These can be organized in most cities along the Trans-Siberian for US$35-60/£20-35 /€30-50 per person per night including some or all meals, with additional charges for any tours, ticketing, transport or other services. A reliable agency is Host Families Association in St Petersburg (HOFA; 🖥 www .hofa.ru); also see p19.

To minimize any misunderstandings, agree in advance on meal times, and on how much you can afford for food if this is not included. When you visit markets it's customary and polite to supplement your host's supplies with ingredients they might not otherwise have or be able to afford.

At some railway stations you may be approached by locals offering to put you up in their houses for around US$10/£5/€8 per night. Look the place over before agreeing, and don't allow yourself to be persuaded if you feel in any way uncomfortable about the arrangement.

Checking in at a hotel

Checking in is never the swift procedure it should be. After the receptionist has kept you waiting for a while, serving other customers and occasionally glancing at you, you'll be asked to hand over your passport to have a stamped piece of paper stapled to it, thus registering you in that city. Alternatively the receptionist may simply add a stamp to a piece of paper that another hotel has already stapled into your passport. You'll then be handed a small pass-card. You must present this to the *dezhurnaya* (floor attendant) on your floor in exchange for your room key; in some hotels you may be given your key by the receptionist.

The *dezhurnaya*, often an elderly female busybody, seems to spend most of her time drinking tea in a little den, gossiping with friends and keeping an eagle eye on all that happens on her floor. She usually turns very friendly when she figures out that you are a foreigner. As with *provodniks* on the trains, it's wise to keep on good terms with her. She can provide boiling water or mineral water at all hours and arrange to get laundry done.

Most hotels have a midday check-out time, but you can usually pay for a couple of extra hours or a half day if your train leaves in the evening.

Bedrooms

Rooms are vast and comfortable in some older hotels but rather smaller in more modern places. Mid-range hotels are generally furnished in the worst possible taste, often verging on the schizophrenic: pink roses on the wallpaper matched with purple nylon curtains. Beds are often too short, usually of orthopaedic hardness or so old that every spring digs into you. Bedding, usually consisting of blankets in a duvet cover, is always clean though sometimes a bit threadbare.

There's usually an internal phone and wake-up calls may be arranged at the reception desk; these seem to be reliable and often the *dezhurnaya* will knock on your door as well to make sure. You may get phone calls to your room in the evening from women offering 'personal services'; a firm 'no' usually ends the calls.

Bathrooms

Most places now provide toilet paper, soap and a clean towel or two. Bathrooms are usually clean but, except in smarter hotels, tend to be in poor repair. Sink and bath plugs are rare, so it's wise to carry your own universal plug.

It may take a minute or so before the tap water comes out hot. Hot water is centrally supplied and because pipes need an annual cleaning, your hotel and every other building in the city may be without hot water for up to four weeks (more in some Siberian cities) during the summer. Only some top-end hotels with independent hot-water systems may escape this. Don't expect a discount on your bill just because you don't have hot water.

TOURS

While guided tours allow you to cover a lot of ground quickly, you can easily get around by yourself in all the cities in this book. You'll learn far more on the buses and metro than you will inside a tour bus. There are some tours that are worth going on, though, and these are mentioned in the relevant city section of this book.

If you fancy a tour of Moscow, St Petersburg and Golden Ring cities there's a backpacker tour bus to take you around: the Beetroot Bus (UK ☎ 020-8566 8846, 🖳 www.beetroot.org).

LOCAL TRANSPORT

If you're booking an independent trip through an agency, you may be encouraged to purchase 'transfers' so that you will be met at the airport or station on arrival and taken to your hotel. Prices tend to be high (typically US$40-80/£25-45 /€32-65, depending on distance) but it can be money well spent: if you intend to take a taxi from the airport in particular, it may be worth booking a transfer instead, if only to keep yourself out of the hands of the taxi mafia.

Taxis

Virtually every car in Russia is a taxi: stand in the street with your arm outstretched and someone will pull over and ask where you want to go. Negotiate a price and get in. It's illegal, but if drivers are going your way it makes sense for them to take paying passengers. But while this may be very convenient it can also be dangerous, as you have no idea of the driver's intentions. Women travelling alone would be unwise to hitch rides, and no one should get into a car that has more than one occupant. Don't put your luggage in the boot (trunk) or your driver could simply pull away when you get out to retrieve it. Russians seem to delight in worrying about crime and if you ask them they'll tell you numerous stories about unwary passengers being driven into the countryside and robbed.

Official taxis are safer. You'll recognize them by the green 'for hire' light. Although they have meters, few use them. You should agree on a price before you even get in since once the driver realizes you're a foreigner, he'll bump it up accordingly. Ask a local beforehand what the taxi trip should cost and don't be afraid to haggle; even if you haven't a clue, at least get the price down a bit. You'll find that taxi drivers stick together and one won't offer you a lower price than the others. You're more likely to be charged local rates if you don't pick up taxis outside big hotels or major tourist spots.

Metro

The metro is a very cheap way to get around, with a flat fare in Moscow of R15 and trains every few minutes. In Moscow it's worth using the metro just to see the stations, which are more like subterranean stately homes, with ornate ceilings, gilded statues and enormous chandeliers.

Be careful boarding metro-station escalators as they move about twice as fast as Western ones. Russian metro stations are deeper underground than their Western counterparts in order to double as bomb shelters, so their escalators are long and swift. The one at St Petersburg's Ploshchad Lenina station rises 59m (194ft).

At street level, metro stations are indicated by a large blue or red 'M'. Lines are named after their terminal stations, as on the Paris metro. Where two lines intersect, the transfer station may have two names, one for each line. As trains move off from the station, the next station is announced. The counter above the end of each tunnel indicates how long it's been since the last train left. In Siberia there are metros in Novosibirsk and Yekaterinburg.

Buses

Every major city has a bus service (fixed-fare and often very crowded) and usually also trolley-buses and trams. Some buses have conductors, some have ticket machines and in others tickets are purchased from the driver in strips or booklets. If there's no conductor you must validate your own ticket, using one of the punches by the windows. If the bus is crowded and you can't reach, pass your ticket to someone near a punch and they'll do it for you. Occasionally, inspectors impose on-the-spot fines for those without punched tickets.

Domestic flights

Domestic flights usually involve long delays and far too much sitting around in airports. Safety standards are not high: if you must fly use one of the larger carriers such as Aeroflot or Transaero. Many hotels have airline ticket booking offices.

Boat

Most of the cities you will visit are built on rivers and short trips on the water are usually possible. In St Petersburg the most interesting way to reach Petrodvorets is by hydrofoil. From Irkutsk you can get to Lake Baikal by boat up the Angara River. There are also some long-distance options: for example, a four-day trip up the Yenisey from Krasnoyarsk to Dudinka.

Car rental

In St Petersburg, Moscow and some other cities it is possible to rent self-drive cars. Charges start at about US$50/£30 /€40 a day, and you need an international driving licence. You're unlikely to be allowed to drive east of the Urals.

BUYING RAIL TICKETS

Classes of service

There are four main classes of service on Russian trains. **Obshchy** (meaning general) signifies carriages with unreserved seating only. **Platskartny** (3rd class) is the most basic of sleeping carriages, an open-plan arrangement of doorless compartments, each with four bunks in tiers of two plus another bunk beside the corridor. **Kupé** (coupé; also called 2nd, hard or tourist class) refers to carriages with four-berth closed compartments. **SV** (*spalny vagon*, literally 'sleeping car'; also called 1st or soft class) has comfortable, two-berth compartments which sometimes have washbasins. Some Trans-Siberian trains have an additional **deluxe 1st class** (see p119).

The term *firmenny* refers not to carriages but to certain train services, including all international trains and many domestic ones. On firmenny trains you can expect extra attention to detail and comfort in all classes.

❑ 'Whilst admittedly my longest stint on this trip was about 55 hours, I always use Platskartny wherever possible on price basis. Sure, the extra space/comfort might be nice, a lot of the people who do trips like this are on tight budgets and are more than willing to put up with Plats for the savings'. **(Rich Perkins**, UK)

❑ BUYING A TRAIN TICKET

Within Russia you will probably want a ticket for travel either the same day or within a couple of days. In either case it's usually possible to go to the station or ticket office, find the correct window, buy your ticket and be out again fairly quickly. If you don't speak Russian you can use the form on p74. Payment is in rouble cash only.

Which train?

The timetable displayed in the booking hall states the train's number, the time of departure and the days on which it travels.

● The train number indicates its direction, with even numbers indicating generally eastbound or northbound travel, and odd numbers westbound or southbound.

● Timetables invariably use Moscow Time. Across a network covering eight time zones this is the only way the system could work. The clock in the booking hall is normally set to Moscow Time. Some station clocks have two hour-hands, black for local time and red for Moscow Time.

● Most trains depart daily, but some run only on odd-numbered days of each month (1st, 3rd, 5th etc) and some only on even-numbered days.

Which ticket window?

There are usually several ticket windows (*kassa* касса) depending on your destination and possibly on whether you want a same-day or advance-purchase ticket. Staff may not always be very helpful. If the choice is not obvious, go to the administrator's window (Администртор) where you'll either be sold a ticket or told where to get one. If there's a queue and you want to return later, take note of the window's closing times.

Stations in most major cities have 'service centres' with staff who speak a smattering of English. At these centres you must pay a small extra service fee of up to US$7.

Which ticket?

At the window you'll need to tell them your destination, train number, date of departure and compartment class: Л (L = two-berth *SV*), M (M = four-berth *SV*), K (K = *kupé*), П (P = *platskartny*), O (O = *obshchi*), either verbally or in writing (see opposite). There are several types of long-distance tickets but the most common is a long computer-printed one (see opposite). It contains not only information about the train but also your name and passport number (so don't buy someone else's ticket from them). If you're buying for someone else you have to present their passport. The only way for a ticket to be legally renamed once it is bought is for the ticket seller to cover the original name with an official sticker and write your name on it.

On the train the conductor tears the ticket, which prevents it being used again. If your ticket is for a train originating somewhere other than your own boarding station, you may get a berth number only after you board the train.

Prices

Overnight rail tickets in Russia are considerably cheaper than in the West; a kupé ticket for a 24-hour journey costs about US$60/£35/€50. Supply varies, and the official response appears to be to raise prices when demand seems to be exceeding supply.

TICKET BUYING FOR NON-RUSSIAN SPEAKERS

If you can't speak enough Russian to buy a ticket write what you need on a piece of paper as shown below. The clerk will usually write down a suggested train number and departure time and hand it back to you. Say *Da* (Yes) and you'll get the ticket. Check that the time the clerk writes down is Moscow Time by pointing to it and saying *Moskovskoye vremya*?

For more complex enquiries use the form on p74. If there's a long queue, however, it would be better to transcribe the question you need answered from the page opposite onto a piece of paper rather than trying to get the clerk to look through the whole page.

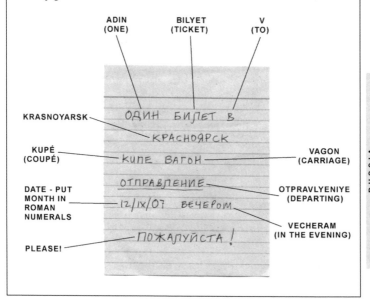

RUSSIA

The ticket price comprises a booking fee (US$4 to US$20 depending on where you buy the ticket) plus a charge depending upon the class of service and the distance travelled. Most popular for overnight journeys is the four-berth *kupé* ticket. A two-berth *SV* ticket is generally 1.5 to 2 times the cost of kupé, and tickets for firmenny trains cost about 1.2 to 1.5 times non-firmenny tickets.

Stations in Moscow or St Petersburg will issue domestic tickets up to 45 days in advance and international tickets up to 40 days ahead. Larger stations elsewhere may only allow 30 days' advance purchase. Locals can hold reservations without paying until 10 days before departure, at which point unsold tickets are released and resold.

RUSSIA

TRAIN INFORMATION AND TICKET BUYING FORM

Please help me.
Будте любезны, помогите мне.

I don't speak Russian.
Я не говорю по-русски.

Please read the question I point to and write the answer or...
Прочтите вопросы на которые я укажу, и напишите ответ

* = circle your choice.
Или * = кружите свой выбор.

Q = question / A = answer
Воп. = вопрос / Отв. = ответ

MT = Moscow Time
МВ = Московское Время

Information / Информация

Q. When is the next train with available SV* kupé* platskartny* spaces to ....?
Воп. Когда следующий поезд со свободными местами (СВ* купе* плацкарт*) до ....?

A. The train No. is ....
It departs at .... : .... (MT).
Отв. Номер у поезда ....
Отправляется в .... : ....(МВ).

Q. Are there SV* kupé* platskartny* tickets to ....
on train No. ....?
Воп. Есть свободные места (СВ* купе* плацкарт*) до ....
в поезде номер ....?

A. Yes / No
Отв. Да / Нет

Q. When does the train depart and arrive?
Воп. Когда поезд отправляется и прибывает?

A. It departs at .... : .... and arrives at .... : .... (MT).
Отв. Отправляется в .... : ....
и прибывает в .... : .... (МВ).

Q. How much does a SV* kupé* platskartny* ticket cost?
Воп. Сколько стоит билет в СВ* купе* плацкарт*?

A. It costs .... roubles.
Отв. Билет стоит .... рублей.

Q. Which ticket window should I go to?
Воп. К какой кассе мне подойти?

A. Ticket window No. ....
Отв. Касса номер ....

Q. What platform does train No. .... leave from?
Воп. С какой платформы отправляется поезд номер ....?

A. Platform No. ....
Отв. Платформа номер ....

Buying tickets / Покупка билетов

Q. May I buy .... SV* kupé* platskartny* tickets to ....
on train No. ..... leaving on ....?
(DD/MM/YY format, eg 31/12/00.)
Воп. Можно купить ... (СВ* купе* плацкарт*) билет до ....
на поезд номер .... который отправляется до ....?

A. Yes, it costs .... roubles.
Отв. Да. Билет стоит .... рублей.

A. No.
Отв. Нет.

Q. Why can't I buy a ticket?
Воп. Почему я не могу купить билет?

A. There is no train.
Отв. Нет поезда.

A. The train is fully booked.
Отв. Нет мест.

A. You must buy your ticket at window No. ....
Отв. Вы должны купить билет в кассе номер..............

A. You can only buy a ticket .... hours before the train arrives.
Отв.Вы можете купить билет за .... часов до прибытия поезда.

Thank you for your help.
Большое спасибо за помощь.

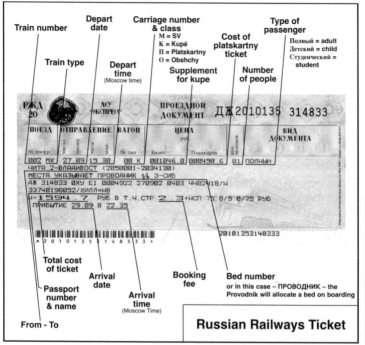

Russian Railways Ticket

Labels around the ticket:
- Train number
- Depart date
- Carriage number & class — M = SV, K = Kupé, П = Platskartny, O = Obshchy
- Cost of platskartny ticket
- Type of passenger — Полный = adult, Детский = child, Студенческий = student
- Train type
- Depart time (Moscow time)
- Supplement for kupe
- Number of people
- Total cost of ticket
- Passport number & name
- From - To
- Arrival date
- Arrival time (Moscow Time)
- Booking fee
- Bed number — or in this case – ПРОВОДНИК – the Provodnik will allocate a bed on boarding

RUSSIA

Getting off in the middle of a journey

It is possible to break your journey once on any through ticket, but it's hardly worth the effort. You must get the stationmaster to validate your ticket within 30 minutes of arrival, then re-book a berth for the onward journey (which can often be done only by the chief ticket officer). If you don't speak Russian, don't even attempt this.

Buying a ticket with 'built-in' stopovers is almost as difficult. Most ticket sellers will advise you to wait and buy tickets for onward segments at your stopover towns. However you may find that sleeping berth reservations are in short supply at smaller stations, so think twice before stopping off at obscure villages or towns.

ELECTRICITY

In almost all Russian cities electricity is 220V, 50 cycle AC. Sockets require a continental-type plug or adaptor. In some places the voltage is 127V so you should enquire at the reception desk before using your own appliances. Sockets for electric razors are provided on trains but these days Russians mostly use them to charge mobile phones.

TIME

Russia spans eight time zones, and on the Trans-Siberian you will be adjusting your watch by an hour almost every day. Russian railways run entirely on Moscow Time, and timetables do not list local time. It can be disconcerting to cross the border from China at breakfast-time, only to be informed by station clocks that it's just 02:00.

Moscow Time (MT) is four hours ahead of Greenwich Mean Time when the country is on 'summer time': from the last Sunday in March to the last Saturday in October. Outside that period MT = GMT+3. Siberian local time zones are listed throughout the route guide; those for the main cities are: Novosibirsk (MT+3), Irkutsk (MT+5), Khabarovsk (MT+7) and Vladivostok (MT+7).

MONEY

(See also p46). The basic unit of Russian currency is the rouble, which is divided into 100 kopecks. There are 1, 5, 10 and 50-kopeck and 1, 2, 5 and 10-rouble coins; banknotes come in denominations of 10, 50, 100, 500 and 1000 roubles. When the currency was devalued in 1998 by a factor of 1000, all old notes ceased to be legal tender.

The use of US dollars is illegal in Russia with a few exceptions including airline ticket sales and visa fees. Upmarket hotels and restaurants may quote prices in US$ or euros but will expect payment in roubles. Some Russians still change their roubles to dollars for security, although as the rouble stabilizes they are gaining confidence in their own currency.

What to bring

Euros and US dollars are the easiest currencies to exchange throughout Russia. UK pounds and a few other non-EU currencies can be changed in Moscow and St Petersburg, and Swedish kroner and Finnish marks in St Petersburg. Japanese yen are easily exchanged in Khabarovsk and Vladivostok.

Foreign banknotes should be as new, crisp and clean as possible. US dollar notes should be dated 1996 or later, as these provide good protection against counterfeiting. Every foreign banknote you exchange will be examined closely and older ones, especially if they're torn, soiled or have writing or ink stamps on them, are likely to be rejected, especially in smaller towns. Your bank at home may hate you for insisting on clean, new notes but it will save you many headaches on the road.

Cashing travellers' cheques is nearly impossible outside weekday banking hours, and difficult at any time outside larger cities. If you do decide to bring travellers' cheques, you will have the fewest problems with American Express cheques denominated in US dollars.

Exchanging money

You'll have no problem finding somewhere to change money as there are hundreds of official currency-exchange offices (*obmen valyuty*) in hotels, banks, stores and kiosks in most cities. The difference in banks' buying and selling rates is about 2-4%. Rates at currency-exchange offices may vary according to supply and demand and whether banks are open. Out of hours you will get a worse deal than during bank hours.

You may have difficulty getting change back from R1000 notes in smaller shops. It's always good to keep a stash of coins and small-denomination rouble notes.

❏ Exchange rates	
To get the latest rates of exchange visit 🖳 www.xe.com.	
US$1	R25.90
UK£1	R51.72
Euro €1	R34.80
Aus $1	R21.90
Can $1	R24.20
China Y10	R33.40
Japan ¥100	R21.00
Mong T1000	R22.25
NZ$1	R19.85
Sing$1	R16.83
S Africa R10	R36.50

Credit/debit cards and ATMs
Credit cards – especially Visa and MasterCard, less readily American Express and Diners Club – are now accepted in many of Russia's upmarket shops, hotels and restaurants. In most cities, including those along the Trans-Siberian it's easy to find ATMs where a range of debit cards can be used for rouble cash advances. ATMs are so plentiful that you can confidently rely on debit cards for almost all your money needs, though you'll want a supply of cash for emergencies.

The black market
With little difference between bank rates and black market rates, the risks involved in changing money this way far outweigh the benefits. There's also nothing to be gained from bringing in Western goods to sell, since almost everything can now be bought locally.

Tipping
Soviet policy outlawed tipping, seen as nothing less than bribery: the thin end of the corruption wedge. Now it's made a comeback, though you'll be seen as ostentatious if you tip at Western levels. Russians generally give up to 10% in restaurants. Porters expect about US$1 and guides US$5-10 per day. There is no need to tip taxi drivers.

POST AND TELECOMMUNICATIONS
Email
Internet access is widespread in Russia. There are internet cafés in every city covered in this book (see the City Guides chapter for locations). New ones are opening all the time; check the locations at 🖳 www.cybercafes.com. Access costs US$1-2 per hour in most places.

Post
Airmail to and from the UK and USA takes about two weeks and is generally reliable. Letters may be opened in transit by thieves looking for money, so don't send anything valuable or important in either direction. To send a parcel from Russia you must have it wrapped and sealed with a wax stamp at the post office.

On international mail to and from Russia, addresses may be written in English and in standard Western format. For domestic mail the usual format is the following, and should be all in Russian:

> Six-digit postal code
> Name of city or town
> Street name, with house number set off by a comma
> Name of addressee
> followed below by the return address.

On international mail it is helpful to write the country name in Cyrillic:

> UK: **Великобритания**, USA: **США**
> Canada: **Канада**, Germany: **Германия**
> Australia: **Австралия**, New Zealand: **Новая Зеландия**

If you wish to send something urgent or valuable out of Russia you should use one of the courier companies such as DHL that have branches around Russia.

Telephone

The Russian telephone system has greatly improved, and it's relatively easy to dial into or out of the country. To make an international call dial 8, then wait for a secondary tone and dial 10 followed by the country code and number. Note that in 2007 or early 2008 this will change to 0 followed by 00.

To call from a street telephone (*taksofon*) you need a prepaid telephone card (*kartochka dlya taksofona*); these are available from kiosks and metro station ticket windows. When placing a call from a taksofon it's important to remember that, as soon as the other party answers, you must press a button to 'start' the call; otherwise you cannot be heard! This button can be a separate button on the telephone, or a number (usually the number 3).

However, taksofon cards are only useful for local calls. For intercity and international calls you should purchase one of a variety of international cards printed with a toll-free or local-rates telephone number and a PIN number. These cards are widely available in shops and kiosks and all have similar rates. To navigate voice prompts with these cards your telephone must have '*' and '#' keys. Most Russian telephones are pulse-dial so you must switch to tone-dial after being connected, usually by pressing '*'. Some cards have a further option for English-language voice prompts.

You can also make calls from telephone offices, usually part of the post office. Leave a deposit with the cashier who will assign you a booth from which you make your call. Pay the balance after the call.

Upper-end hotels in most Russian cities may also have telephones which take credit/debit cards or the hotel's own brand of card, but calls from such telephones tend to be very expensive.

For information on bringing a mobile phone to Russia, see p44.

Fax

The main city post offices often have public fax machines, with typical international rates of around US$5/£3 per minute (one to two pages).

MAGAZINES AND NEWSPAPERS

Two free, visitor-friendly, English-language newspapers worth looking out for in their respective cities are the daily *Moscow Times* and the twice-weekly *St Petersburg Times*. They're easy to find in hotels, hostels, cafés and supermarkets frequented by foreigners.

Western news magazines such as *Time* and *Newsweek* are sold at better hotels.

PUBLIC HOLIDAYS

National holidays

If a holiday falls on Thursday, Friday and Saturday may also be holidays. If a holiday falls on Saturday or Sunday, Monday will be a holiday.

- 1 January: New Year's Day
- 7 January: Russian Orthodox Christmas Day
- 13 January: New Year's Day according to the old Julian calendar
- 15 February: Defenders of the Motherland Day
- 8 March: International Women's Day
- Late April/early May: Russian Orthodox Easter
- 1 May: Day of Spring and Labour (formerly May Day or International Working People's Solidarity Day). The following work day is also a holiday.
- 9 May: Victory Day, commemorating the end of World War II (known in Russia as the 1941-45 Great Patriotic War)
- 12 June: Independence Day for Russia
- 7-8 November: Grief Day or Reconciliation Day (formerly the Anniversary of the October Revolution)
- 12 December: Constitution Day

School and university holidays

Schools start 1 September and finish 31 May with a week's vacation in November, two weeks in January at the New Year and one week in March. Universities usually start on 1 September and finish on 25 June with the winter break from 25 January to 8 February.

FESTIVALS

Annual arts festivals in Moscow include Moscow Stars (5-15 May) and Russian Winter (25 December to 5 January).

The most interesting festival is St Petersburg's White Nights, held around the summer solstice, when the sun does not set. The days are separated by only a few hours of silvery light: a combined dusk and dawn. Theatres and concert halls save their best performances for this time and a festival is also held at Petrodvorets.

FOOD AND DRINK

There's more to Russian cuisine than borscht and chicken Kiev, but if you eat most of your meals on the train you'll have little chance to discover this. You'll probably leave with the idea that Russian cooking is of the school-dinner variety, with large hunks of meat, piles of potatoes and one vegetable (the interminable cabbage), followed by tinned fruit or ice cream. On the whole Russian cuisine is bland, but you will occasionally be surprised by the delicious food which seems to appear in the most unlikely restaurants.

When Russians eat at home, the first meal of the day consists of fruit juice (good if it's apple), cheese, eggs, sausage, bread, jam and *kefir* (thin, sour yoghurt). Lunch and dinner will be of a similarly large size, each consisting of at least three courses. In restaurants, however, portions are considerably smaller than in the West.

Zakuski

Russian hors d'oeuvres (*zakuski*) consist of some or all of the following: cold meat, sausages, salmon, pickled herring, paté, tomato salad, sturgeon and caviare. Large quantities of vodka are drunk with zakuski.

Soups

Soups are on the watery side but tasty and make meals in themselves with a stack of brown bread. Best known is *borscht* (beetroot soup) which often includes other vegetables (potatoes, cabbage and onion), chopped ham and a swirl of *smetane* (sour cream).

Shchi (cabbage soup) is the traditional soup of the proletariat and was a favourite of Nicholas II, who is said to have enjoyed only plain peasant cooking, to the great disappointment of his French chef. *Akroshka* is a chilled soup

---

Caviare
The roe of the sturgeon is becoming more expensive as the fish itself becomes rarer. Four species are acknowledged to produce the best caviare: beluga, sterlet, osetra and sevruga, all of them from the Caspian and Black Seas. To produce caviare's characteristic flavour (preferably not too 'fishy') a complicated process is involved. The female sturgeon is stunned with a mallet, her belly slit open and the roe sacs removed. The eggs are washed and strained into batches of uniform size. The master-taster then samples the roe and decides how much salt to add for preservation.

Processed caviare varies in colour (black, red or golden) and also in the size of the roe. It is either eaten with brown bread or served with sour cream in *blinis* (thin pancakes). If you want it you can get it in most tourist hotels and on the train.

A recent report from the World Wide Fund for Nature warns that the sturgeon is on the brink of extinction because of aggressive fishing by Russia. The report says that up to 90% of caviare is now obtained illegally and that Russian authorities are doing nothing because of corruption.

You don't eat meat?!

Vegetarian cooking isn't widely understood in Russia and with the exception of one or two Hare Krishna-style Asian restaurants, there are no genuinely vegetarian restaurants. Vegetarians can manage in Russian restaurants if they choose carefully, but they shouldn't rely on the waiter's imagination or assistance!

Amongst **appetizers**, *shchi* (cabbage soup) is often meatless; suluguni cheese is very similar to Greek halloumi and usually served grilled; and carrot, tomato and cucumber salads are also available.

Main courses are harder; one option is to order a double portion of a starter found on almost every Russian menu: *Julienne*, also known as *griby v smetane* – wild mushrooms baked in cream sauce. Omelettes are another option, if a horribly predictable one. Perversely, you can often do better in cheap cafés than in fine restaurants because meatless food is regarded as rather down-market. Items to look for in cafés are *piroshkie* (dough-pastries with fillings like onion, cabbage or carrot), *vatrushkie* (cream-cheese pastries) and *vareniki* (cheese-filled dumplings). You can almost always find *blini* or *oladi* (different kinds of Russian pancakes) served with either sour cream or jam. In Georgian restaurants *lobio* (spicy bean stew) is a vegetarian mainstay, and a few Georgian places also serve *achma* (a kind of cream-sauce lasagne) – combined with *khachapuri* cheesebreads and some salads, this is about as good as it gets.

Neil McGowan

of meat, vegetables and *kvas* (a beer-like brew made from fermented bread). *Rassolnik* is a soup of pickled vegetables.

Fish

Fish common in Russia include herring, halibut, salmon and sturgeon. These last two may be served with a creamy vegetable sauce. In Irkutsk you should try *omul*, the famous Lake Baikal fish, which has a delicious, delicate flavour.

Meat

The most famous Russian main course is chicken Kiev (fried breast of chicken filled with garlic and butter). Almost as famous is *boeuf* Stroganov (named after the wealthy merchant family who financed the first Siberian explorations in the 1580s), a beef stew made with sour cream and mushrooms.

Other regional specialities you're likely to encounter include *shashlyk* (mutton kebabs) and *plov* (rice with mutton and spices) from Central Asia, chicken *tabaka* (with garlic sauce) from Georgia, and a Ukrainian dish worth avoiding at all costs, *salo* or pig's fat preserved with salt, said to be good for hangovers.

From Siberia comes *pelmeni*, small meat-filled dumplings served in a soup or as a main course.

If you're expecting a rump steak when you order *bifstek* you'll be disappointed: it's just a compressed lump of minced meat, usually swimming in grease and grey in colour.

Buying your own food

Russian supermarkets *(universam)* generally have everything you would expect a supermarket to have, though except for in the big cities, the selection is slimmer than in the West. Canned and packaged goods, juices, pots, tableware, soap, paper products and dry goods, as well as meat, bread, fruit and vegetables, can be found here.

Produkty stores sell a limited range of fresh vegetables, fruit, bread, meat, eggs and manufactured products. A *gastronome* is a delicatessen; a *dieta* sells products for diabetics and others on special diets. These can all be awkward places for a foreigner to shop. Because the products are kept behind a counter, you don't get much chance to inspect the merchandise, and if you don't speak Russian, all you can do is point at what you want – a difficult system when items are arrayed behind glass.

Markets *(rynok)* range from clusters of old people selling garden produce at metro exits to large covered markets with dozens of stalls offering everything from home-made honey to dried mushrooms, from meat to imported pineapples.

Puddings

Very often the choice is limited to ice cream (*morozhenoye* – always good, safe and available everywhere) and fruit compote (a disappointing fruit salad of a few pieces of tinned fruit floating in a large dish of syrup). You may, however, be offered delicious *blinis* (thin pancakes, like crêpes) with sour cream and fruit jam; *vareniki* (sweet dumplings filled with cheese or fruit) or rice pudding. Unless you are staying in one of the more expensive hotels there won't be much fresh fruit on offer, although it is now easily available from street vendors.

Bread

Russian bread, served with every meal, is wholesome and filling. Tourist brochures boast that over 100 different types are baked in Moscow. Soviet-era

❏ Food and drink prices

Only a few products, such as bread, milk and eggs, are still subsidized and regulated. Some examples of current prices:

Hot dog	US$0.60	Russian beer (500ml bottle)	US$0.85
McDonald's Big Mac	US$1.50	Cheap vodka (1 litre)	US$4.00
Large loaf of white bread	US$0.50	Gostinniy Dvor vodka (1 litre)	US$7.00
Sweet cake	US$0.90	Georgian red wine (1 litre)	US$6.50
Russian 'Edam' style cheese (1kg)	US$5.00	Sekt Russian champagne (1 litre)	US$5.00
Large jar Nutella spread	US$2.00		

When you buy **vodka** check the seal on the bottle to make sure it hasn't been diluted. It's wise to go for the bigger brands: some smaller distilleries reportedly cut costs by producing low-grade alcohol, which has resulted in blindness and death amongst some drinkers.

Drinking water
Although tap water is safe to drink in most Russian cities, it's wise to stick to bottled mineral water or boiled water. At all costs, avoid tap water in St Petersburg since it may be infected with giardia, which can cause a nasty and persistent form of diarrhoea. In Irkutsk and Listvyanka you can safely drink the tap water, which comes directly from Lake Baikal.

On the train, boiled water is always available from samovars in each carriage.

In Mongolia and China, drink only boiled or bottled water; thermos flasks of boiled water are routinely provided on trains and in hotels. Tap water is safe in Japan and Hong Kong.

'bread technology' was allegedly in such great demand in the West that Russian experts were recruited to build a brown-bread factory in Finland. If you're packing for the train, note that brown bread stays fresh much longer than white bread, which goes stale after a day or two.

Drinks
Non-alcoholic Most popular is tea, traditionally served black with a spoonful of jam or sugar. Milk is not always available so you may want to take along some powdered creamer. Russians have been brewing coffee since Peter the Great introduced it in the 17th century, but standards have dropped since then. Even a jar of instant coffee from home may taste better.

Bottled mineral water is available everywhere, often carbonated and frequently tasting rather strongly of all those natural minerals that are supposed to be so good for you. There are several varieties of bottled fruit juice (*sok*), of which apple seems to be the most consistently good.

Alcohol
In a land synonymous with vodka, you may be surprised by the amount of beer-drinking that goes on. It's common to see people, young and old, nursing a bottle on the street, or even on public transport, at all hours of the day. Russian beer is cheap and readily available and the most popular brands, including Baltika, Bochka and Bochkarev, are of a high standard.

Vodka still predominates, of course, and Russians will be disgusted if you do anything other than drink it straight. The spirit originated in Poland (although some say that it was brought back from Holland by Peter the Great) and means 'little water', something of an understatement. If you tire of the original product, there's a range of flavoured vodkas to sample, including lemon, cherry, blackberry and pepper.

Be warned that the standard vodka measure in Russia is *sto gram* (100g), compared to 25g in the UK. Vodka is traditionally served ice cold and drained in one go from a shot glass. Men are expected to keep this up but a woman might be permitted to drop out after a couple of shots. It can be easy enough to drink but it will quickly catch up with you. You may be asked to give a toast and you should take this seriously – a short speech about your subject is enough.

❑ RUSSIAN CUSTOMS AND ETIQUETTE

Customs

● Wine, cake, candy or flowers are traditional gifts if you're invited to dinner in someone's home. A small gift for any children is also appropriate. If you bring flowers be sure the number of flowers is uneven: even numbers are for funerals.

● Shaking hands or kissing across the threshold of a doorstep is considered to bring bad luck.

● Take off your gloves when shaking hands.

● Be prepared to remove your shoes upon entering a home. You will be given a pair of slippers (*tapki*) to help keep the apartment clean.

● Do not cross your legs with the ankle on the knee, as it's impolite to show people the soles of your shoes. When in the metro or sitting on a bus, don't let your feet even come close to a seat or to another passenger.

● Smoking is common and accepted in Russia.

● Be prepared to accept all alcohol and food offered when visiting friends, and this can be quite a lot. Refusing a drink or a toast is a serious breach of etiquette. An open bottle must be finished.

● Be prepared to give toasts at dinners, etc. Be careful, the vodka can catch up with you.

● Dress up for the theatre. Check in your coat and any large bags at the garderobe.

● Be careful how you admire something in a home. Your host may offer it to you to take away.

● Russian men still expect women to act in a traditional manner. It's bad form for a woman to be assertive in public, to carry heavy bags if you're walking with a man, to open doors, uncork bottles or pay your own way in social situations. A woman alone in a restaurant or hotel risks being taken for a prostitute.

● Dress casually for dinner in someone's home. Wear a hat in cold weather, or babushkas will lecture you on your foolishness!

● In a Russian Orthodox church women should cover their heads with a scarf or hat and wear a skirt. Men should remove their hats.

● Putting your thumb between your first two fingers is a very rude gesture.

Superstitions

Russians remain remarkably superstitious; many of the following were once also common elsewhere in Europe:

● Never light a cigarette from a candle. It will bring you bad luck.

● Do not whistle indoors or you will whistle away your money.

● Never pour wine back-handed, it means you will also pour away your money.

● A black cat crossing your path is bad luck.

● A woman who finds herself sitting at the corner of a table will be single for the next seven years.

● If you spill salt at the table you will be plagued by bad luck unless you immediately throw three pinches over your left shoulder.

● If someone offers you good wishes, or if you are discussing your good fortune, you must spit three times over your left shoulder and touch (knock on) wood to keep your good fortune.

Note that a shot of vodka ought to be followed immediately by zakuski (see p80): a popular Russian saying is that 'only drunkards drink without food'. Another goes: 'Drinking vodka without beer is like throwing money to the wind'. If someone flicks their throat with their forefinger, it usually means 'How about a drink?'. It's considered impolite to refuse.

If you're buying your own vodka, stick with popular brands like Gzhelka. Cheap vodka from street kiosks is often bootleg and drinking it could give you much worse than a bad hangover. There's also wine: most varieties tend to be rather sweet for the Western palate, but Georgian wines are worth trying. Russian champagne can be surprisingly good if you specify that you want it dry and it's very cheap.

You should also try *kvas* (a beer-like, fermented mixture of stale brown bread, yeast, malt sugar and water). A popular summer cooler sold on the streets from yellow tankers, its alcohol content is so low as to be unnoticeable.

WHERE TO EAT

Russians who can afford to do so take great pleasure in dining out; it's not unusual to find favoured local restaurants completely booked for an entire evening by one family or party. Even in Siberia, there are restaurants as good as in any Western city. Not surprisingly, prices in top places are also a match for those in the West.

The cheapest places to eat are **self-service cafés** (*stolovaya*), where a filling but stodgy meal of salad, bread, potatoes, meat and tea costs about US$2. In many cities there are also Western **fast-food chains** such as McDonald's (recommended at least for their clean loos), plus Russian derivatives such as Russkoye Bistro. In Moscow, St Petersburg and a few other large cities, **cafés** are good places for an interesting and still reasonably cheap meal.

In **restaurants**, service varies wildly: sometimes it's a struggle to get anyone to notice you, while at other times there's a friendly English-speaking waiter or waitress who can't do enough to help you. Staff give guests ample time to interpret the menu and do their best to ensure that no dish arrives too quickly. While you await your food you'll be bombarded by blaring pop radio or the occasional live band. If you get invited to join a Russian party, a visit to a restaurant can be a very entertaining, often drunken affair. Note that tsarist traditions die hard: if a man wishes to invite a woman from another table to dance he must first ask permission of the men at her table.

In some upmarket restaurants you may find cover and/or entertainment charges of up to 10% added to your bill. Sometimes they'll just round up the total by about this amount to save the bother of doing an accurate calculation.

ENTERTAINMENT

Nightlife in Moscow and St Petersburg is as good as you'll get in any big Western city. These cities have lots of nightclubs, discos and bars, but it really helps to have Russian friends to show you the best places. In smaller towns your major options are the hotel bars and discos, which often stay open late. Most provincial cities also have a modern 'megaclub' which combines a disco, bowling alley, bar and restaurant; these places are very popular and pick up late in the evening, but they're sometimes outside the city centre. Casinos you may find difficult to get into and want to leave as soon as you do. Traditional cultural activities such as opera, theatre, ballet or the circus are a better choice. Performances usually start early: between 18:00 and 19:00; don't be late or ushers may not let you in until the interval.

Ballet
Many of the world's greatest dancers have been from Russia's Bolshoi and Kirov companies. Some defected to the West including the Kirov's Rudolf Nureyev, Russia's most famous ballet star, who liked to say he was 'shaken out' of his mother's womb on the Trans-Siberian as it rattled towards Lake Baikal.

Don't miss the chance of a night at the magnificent Bolshoi Theatre; the season runs from September to May. Note that many touring groups dance at the Bolshoi so it may not be the famous company you see.

Opera and theatre
In the past, opera was encouraged more than theatre as it was seen as politically neutral. Glasnost, however, encouraged playwrights to dramatize Russian life as it is, rather than as the government wanted people to see it. This has led to a number of successful new theatre groups opening in Moscow and St Petersburg. There are also several puppet theatres which are highly recommended.

Cinema
In the 1980s the Soviet film industry benefited from the greater freedoms that came with glasnost. In early 1987 one of the most successful and controversial films was *Is It Easy To Be Young?*, which was deeply critical of the Soviet war in Afghanistan. In the 1990s the pessimism of the people towards life is reflected in films made in the country. *Little Vera* (1990) is the story of a provincial girl who sinks into small-time prostitution and finally drowns herself (Gorbachev walked out of it saying he disapproved of the sex scenes). In *Executioner* (1991) a female journalist takes on the mafia in St Petersburg and loses.

The 1994 film *Burnt by the Sun*, by director Nikita Mikhalkov, set in the mid-1930s just before Stalin's Great Purge, won the grand prize at the Cannes Film Festival as well as the Academy Award for best foreign-language film. The 1997 film *Brother*, featuring a sparse crime tale reminiscent of French new wave, signalled a new era in Russian movie-making. Also notable is 2002's dreamlike *Russian Ark* by director Alexander Sokurov. Consisting of a single 90-minute camera shot moving through St Petersburg's Winter Palace, it was the world's second-ever unedited feature film.

Nowadays Western, and especially American, films are everywhere. Every sizeable town has a cinema, with shows starting early in the evening. There is a thriving black market in bootleg American movies; don't be surprised to find *Harry Potter* showing in your restaurant car.

Television

Despite President Putin's crackdown on formerly independent television stations, Russian airwaves still carry news and current affairs programmes of quite high quality. You'll find a smattering of domestic and Western films dubbed in Russian and advertisements can be an interesting window into the local culture. Hotel TVs often have satellite channels, a welcome break from the usual round of garish game-shows.

Rock concerts and sports matches

Rock concerts and sports fixtures are invariably held in stadiums. These are usually well worth attending and very safe as the arenas swarm with police and soldiers to keep order. Football is very popular, as is ice hockey in winter. Tennis has grown in popularity following the emergence of successful Russian tennis players such as Anna Kournikova.

SHOPPING

Shopping in Moscow and St Petersburg is a heady experience, as they boast some of the country's grandest and most luxurious department stores. Here you'll rub shoulders with the new Russian elite, seeking to outdo one another parading their new purchases on Nevsky Prospekt and Kuznetsky Most. Outside these metropolises you'll still find a selection of quality department stores and a handful of fashion shops in each city. Russia takes full advantage of its position straddling Europe and Asia and you'll find no shortage of luxury items as well as cheap imitations. In the electronics section of any department store you'll find quality merchandise on a par with anything available in the West.

Department stores

Department stores (*univermag*) sell a variety of manufactured goods such as clothing, linens, toys, homewares and shoes. No visit to Moscow would be complete without a visit to GUM, Russia's largest department store. It comprises an enormous collection of arcades occupied by upmarket Western chains and boutiques, housed in an impressive glass-roofed building resembling a giant greenhouse. There is another department store chain: TsUM, which has branches in Moscow and most large cities.

Kiosks

Outdoor kiosks are shops in small booths on the sidewalks, squares, markets and around the metros and stations. They often remain open late and a few are open 24 hours. Most sell telephone cards, alcohol, drinks and cigarettes, while others specialize in newspapers, ticket sales, lotto, milk, souvenirs, fruit and vegetables, bootleg CDs and DVDs or clothing.

Opening hours

Large department stores are open from 09:00 to 20:00 Monday to Saturday. Smaller stores have a wide range of opening times, anywhere from 08:00 to 11:00, closing between 20:00 and 23:00. Some shops are closed on Sundays.

What to buy

Handicrafts These include attractively decorated black lacquer *palekh* boxes (icon-painters started making them when religious art lost popularity after the Revolution); enamelled bowls and ornaments; embroidered blouses and table-cloths from the Ukraine; large black printed scarves; guitars and *balalaikas*; lace tablecloths and handkerchiefs; jewellery and gemstones from Siberia and the Urals, and painted wooden ornaments including the ubiquitous *matrioshka* dolls which fit one inside the other. Modern variations on the matrioshka include leaders of the former USSR, the Beatles and even South Park cartoon characters.

Old communist memorabilia have long disappeared from shops but are still sold to tourists and make interesting souvenirs. There is much military memorabilia on sale: anything from hats and hip flasks to diving suits and medals. Check what you're buying carefully as it might not be genuine, and don't declare any of it when you leave Russia. This is equally true with the old bank notes you can buy.

Beware of buying paintings, especially if they are expensive, as duty of 100% or more may be imposed on them when you leave the country. If you are going to buy one, make it a small one so that it will fit into your bag easily. If the painting looks old and potentially valuable, it may well be confiscated by customs officials unless you have a permit from the Ministry of Culture. Customs officials always make a point of looking at paintings when you leave the country.

Books You'll find few English-language books in the shops, but upmarket hotel gift shops usually have a small selection of novels. If you haven't already got one, it's well worth buying an English–Russian/Russian–English dictionary (US$4 or less in most bookshops) to supplement your phrasebook.

Russian-language art books are worth buying for their cheap but usually high-quality reproductions. There are branches of Dom Knigi (House of Books) in Moscow, St Petersburg and most other large cities.

CDs, DVDs and CD-ROMs Pirated Russian and Western music and movies are available everywhere, at around US$3-5 for CDs and US$12 for DVDs; the quality is generally good.

Russian music runs the gamut from pop to metal. Pop groups with staying power over recent years include Ruki Vverkh (Hands Up), Gosti iz Budushchevo (Guests from the Future), Premier Ministr and Ivanushky International. Chai-F is a long-running rock band preferred by older fans. A popular young female vocalist is Alsu. Alla Pugacheva is an older female singer with a loyal following, particularly among women over 40. Newer acts include reggae artists 5nizza, dance-club stars Dr Bronx and Natali, rockers Graydanskaya Oborona, pop artist Lyapis Trubetskoi and punkers Krasnaya Plesen.

CD-ROMs with pirated computer software are widely available, many with English-language versions included. Virtually any application is available, though you need to know what you are looking for. They can be very cheap (as little as US$5), but it's impossible to know what viruses they may contain.

Clothes There is a huge market for fake sports clothes and there are now also dozens of trendy foreign fashion shops in the biggest cities. Russian or old Soviet military clothing is a popular buy for foreigners, but this should be concealed as you leave the country or it may be confiscated.

CRIME

Russia is generally as safe a place to travel as New York or London. But there is an emerging pattern of tourists being singled out for muggings, often violent. Incidents have occurred in small towns as well as big cities across the country. Most of the victims have been men walking alone at night. This seems to happen with increasing frequency as tourism picks up in Russia, so be on guard. When you go out at night, go in a group and if you are on your own take a taxi, even if the distance is short.

Be sensible about your safety. Keep a low profile and don't advertise loudly that you're a foreigner, especially in clubs or bars. Don't dress ostentatiously or wear expensive jewellery. Watch out for pickpockets. Petty pilfering from hotel rooms has also been a problem, you're better off leaving your valuables at home. A money-belt for your passport, credit cards, travellers' cheques and foreign currency is essential. Also see the warnings on p125 for Trans-Siberian travellers.

Mafia racketeering is the crime most often associated with Russia, but the effect on tourists is minimal; mobsters deal in far more money than they could get from you.

In December 2000 gunmen opened fire on the car of Moscow's deputy mayor, Josif Ordzhonikidze, just after he had brokered a deal to open the city's first Formula One racetrack. Seriously injured, he became another statistic confirming that doing business in Russia is dangerous, despite Putin's pledge to establish a 'dictatorship of the law'. There are believed to be over 8000 gangs operating in the country, many of whom, using 'heavies' recruited from the army, extort protection money from businesses. Taxi-drivers have been threatened with having their cars damaged or families attacked. There are even occasional shoot-outs between rival gangs. St Petersburg is considered the most dangerous city in which to operate a business, followed by Moscow and Krasnoyarsk. It seems that it's not the local councils but the mafia who now run Russia's cities.

RUSSIA

Historical outline

EARLY HISTORY

Prehistory: the first Siberians

Discoveries at Dering Yuryakh, by the Lena River 100km south of Yakutsk, have indicated that man has lived in Siberia for far longer than had previously been thought. Archaeologist Yuri Mochanov, who led excavations there in the 1980s and 1990s, believes that the thousands of stone tools he found embedded in geological stratum dating back over two million years suggests human habitation stretching back this far, which would place the site on a par with Professor Leakey's discoveries in East Africa. It's a highly controversial theory as it would mean that initial human evolution also occurred outside Africa. Western archaeologists who have studied the material believe, however, that it cannot be more than 500,000 years old; that would still give the Siberians an impressively long history.

There is evidence of rather more recent human life in the Lake Baikal area. In the 13th millennium BC, Stone Age nomads roamed round the shores of the lake, hunting mammoths and carving their tusks into the tubby fertility goddesses that can be seen in the museums of Irkutsk today. Several sites dating back to this early period have been excavated in the Baikal area; the railway passes near one at the village of Malta (see p389), 85km west of Irkutsk.

There is far more archaeological evidence from the Neolithic Age (12th to 5th millennia BC) and it shows that nomadic tribes had reached the Arctic Circle, with some even moving into North America via the Bering Strait (then a land bridge) and Alaska. These northern nomads trained dogs to pull their sledges, but remained technologically in the Stone Age until Russian colonists arrived in the mid-17th century.

In the south, several Bronze Age cultures emerged around the central parts of the Yenisey River. Afanassevskaya, south of Krasnoyarsk, has given its name to the culture of a people who lived in this area in the 2nd millennium BC and decorated their pottery with a characteristic herringbone pattern.

The first evidence of permanent buildings has been found near Achinsk, where the Andronovo people built huge log cabins in the 1st millennium BC. Excavations of sites of the Karassuk culture, also dated to the 1st millennium BC, have yielded Chinese artifacts, indicating trade between these two peoples.

Early civilizations

The Iron Age sites show evidence of more complex and organized societies. The clear air of the Altai Mountains has preserved the contents of numerous graves of the 2nd century BC Tagar culture. Their leaders were embalmed and buried like Egyptian pharaohs with all that they might need in the afterlife. In their burial mounds archaeologists have found perfectly preserved woollen blankets, decorated leather saddles and the complete skeletons of horses, probably buried alive when their masters died.

In the 3rd century BC the Huns moved into the region south of Lake Baikal where their descendants, the Buryats, now live. The Huns' westward progress continued for five centuries until the infamous Attila, 'The Scourge of God', having pillaged his way across Europe, reached Paris where he was defeated in 452 AD.

The ancestors of the Kyrgyz people were the Tashtyks of Western Siberia, who built large houses of clay (one found near Abakan even has an under-floor central heating system), moulded the features of their dead in clay death masks and decorated their bodies with elaborate tattoos. The tiny Central Asian republic of Kyrgyzstan, south of Kazakhstan, is all that remains of a once mighty empire that stretched from Samarkand to Manchuria in the 12th century.

In the following century the Kyrgyz were defeated by the rapidly advancing Mongols. Genghis Khan's Mongol empire grew to become history's largest land empire, including the Tartars of South Russia and the peoples of North Asia, Mongolia and China.

The first Russian expeditions to Siberia
In mediaeval times Siberia was known to Russians only as a distant land of valuable fur-bearing animals. Occasional expeditions from Novgorod in the 15th century became more frequent in the 16th century, after South Russia was released from the Mongol grip by Tsar Ivan the Terrible. Ivan's seizure of Kazan and Astrakhan opened the way to Siberia. Yediger, leader of a small Siberian kingdom just over the Urals, realized his vulnerability and sent Ivan a large tribute of furs, declaring himself a vassal of the Tsar.

Yediger's son Kuchum was of a more independent mind and, having murdered his father, he put an end to the annual tribute, proclaiming himself Tsar of Siberia. Ivan's armies were occupied on his western frontiers, so he allowed the powerful Stroganov family to raise a private army to annex the rebel lands. In 1574 Ivan granted the Stroganovs a 27-year lease on the land over the Urals as far east as the Tobol River, the centre of Kuchum's kingdom.

Yermak: the founder of Siberia
The Stroganovs' army was a wild bunch of mercenaries led by an ex-pirate named Yermak, the man now recognized as the founder of Siberia. They crossed the Urals and challenged Kuchum, gaining control of his lands after a struggle that was surprisingly long considering that Russian muskets faced only swords and arrows.

On 5 November 1581 Yermak raised the Russian flag at Isker, near modern Tobolsk, and sent the Tsar a tribute of over 2500 furs. In return Ivan pardoned him for his past crimes, sent him a fur-lined cape that had once graced the royal shoulders, and a magnificent suit of armour. Over the next few years Yermak and his men were constantly harassed by Kuchum, and on 16 August 1584 were ambushed as they slept on an island in the Irtysh. The story goes that Yermak drowned in the river, dragged under by the weight of the Tsar's armour. Yermak's name lives on as the top brand of Russian rucksack.

The quest for furs
Over the next 50 years Cossack forces moved rapidly across Siberia, establishing *ostrogs* (military outposts) as they went and gathering tributes of fur for the Tsar. Tyumen was founded in 1586, Tomsk in 1604, Krasnoyarsk in 1628 and Yakutsk in 1633. By 1639 the Cossacks had reached the east coast.

Like the Spanish Conquistadors in South America they dealt roughly with the native tribes they met, who were no match for their muskets and cannon. The prize they lusted after was not gold, as it was for the Spaniards in Peru and for later Russian adventurers in Siberia, but furs. In the days before fur farms, certain pelts were worth far more than they are today; from the proceeds of a season's trapping in Siberia a man could buy and stock a large farm with cattle and sheep. The chances of a Russian trapper finding his way into and out of the dark, swampy forests of the taiga were not very high, but quite a few did it.

Khabarov and the Amur
In 1650 a Russian fur merchant named Khabarov set out from Yakutsk to explore the Amur region in what is now the Far Eastern Territories, fertile and rich in fur-bearing animals. Khabarov found the local tribes extremely hostile, as the Russians' reputation for rape and pillage had spread before him. He and his men committed such atrocities that the news reached the ears of the Tsar, who ordered him back to the capital to explain himself. Bearing gifts of fur, he convinced the Tsar that he had won valuable new lands which would enrich his empire.

The local tribes, however, appealed to the Manchus, their southern neighbours, who sent an army to help them fight off the Russians. The Tsar's men were gradually beaten back. Periodic fighting went on until 1689, when the Russians were forced out of Manchuria and the Amur by the Treaty of Nerchinsk.

18th-century explorers
Peter the Great became Tsar in 1696 and initiated a new era of exploration in the Far East. By the following year the explorer Vladimir Atlasov had claimed Kamchatka for Russia. In 1719 the first scientific expedition set out for Siberia. Peter commissioned the Danish seaman Vitus Bering to search for a northern sea-passage to Kamchatka and the Sea of Okhotsk (unaware that such a route had been discovered by Semyon Deshnev 80 years earlier). However, the Tsar did not live to see Bering set out in 1725.

Between 1733 and 1743 another scientific expedition, comprising naval officers, topographers, geodesic surveyors, naturalists and astronomers, made detailed charts of Russian lands in the Far East. Fur traders reached the Aleutian Islands and in 1784 the first Alaskan colony was founded on Kodiak Island by

Gregory Shelekhov (whose grave is in the cemetery of Znamensky Convent in Irkutsk). Russian Alaska was sold to the United States in 1868 for the bargain price of two cents an acre.

THE 19TH CENTURY

There were two developments in Siberia in the 19th century which had a tremendous effect upon its history. First, the practice of sentencing criminals to a life of exile or hard labour in Siberia was increased to provide labour for the mines and to establish communities around the military outposts. The exile system, which caused a great deal of human misery (see p94), greatly increased the population in this vast and empty region. Secondly, and of far greater importance, was the building of the Trans-Siberian Railway in the 1890s (see p105).

Colonization

By the end of the 18th century the population of Siberia was estimated to be about 1 1/2 million people, most of whom belonged to nomadic native tribes. The policy of populating the region through the exile system swelled the numbers of settlers, but criminals did not make the best colonists. The government therefore tried to encourage voluntary emigration from overcrowded European Russia. Peasant settlers could escape the bonds of serfdom by crossing the Urals, although Siberia's reputation as a place of exile was not much of an incentive to move.

As the railway penetrated Siberia, the transport of colonists was made easier. Tsar Alexander's emigration representatives were sent to many thickly populated regions in European Russia in the 1880s, offering prospective colonists incentives including a reduced rail fare (six roubles for the 1900km/1200-mile journey) and a free allotment of 27 acres of land. Prices in Siberia were high, and colonists could expect to get up to 100% more than in European Russia for produce grown on this land. Many peasants left Europe for Siberia after the great famine of 1890-91.

Further exploration and expansion

Throughout the 19th century scientists and explorers continued to make expeditions to Siberia. In 1829 an expedition led by the German scientist, Baron von Humboldt, already famous for his explorations in South America, investigated the geological structure of the Altai plateau in southern Siberia.

In 1840 the estuary of the Amur was discovered, and colonization was encouraged after Count Muravyev-Amursky, Governor General of Eastern Siberia, annexed the entire Amur territory for Russia, in flagrant violation of the 1689 Russo-Chinese Treaty of Nerchinsk. But the Chinese were in no position to argue, being threatened by the French and English as well as by internal troubles in Peking. By the Treaty of Peking (1860) they ceded the territory north of the Amur to Russia, and also the land east of the Ussuri, including the valuable Pacific port of Vladivostok.

THE EXILE SYSTEM

The word 'Siberia' meant only one thing in Victorian England and 19th century Russia: an inhospitable land of exiled murderers and other evil criminals who paid for their sins by working in its infamous salt mines. While some of the first exiles sent over the Urals did indeed work in salt mines, most of them mined gold, silver or coal.

By 1900 over a million people had been exiled and made the long march to the squalid and overcrowded prisons of Siberia.

George Kennan

In 1891 a book entitled *Siberia and the Exile System*, written by George Kennan, was published in America. It exposed the truly horrific conditions under which prisoners were kept in Siberia and aroused public opinion in both America and Britain. Kennan was a journalist working for the *New York Century Magazine*. He knew Siberia well, having previously spent two years there. At that time he had been unaware of how badly convicts were treated and in a series of lectures before the American Geographical Society had defended the Tsarist government and its exile system.

When his editor commissioned him to investigate the system more thoroughly, bureaucrats in St Petersburg were happy to give him the letters of introduction which allowed him to venture into the very worst of the prisons and to meet the governors and convicts.

The government doubtless hoped that Kennan would champion their cause. Such had been the case with the Rev Dr Henry Landsell who had travelled in Siberia in 1879. In an account of his journey, *Through Siberia*, Landsell wrote that 'on the whole, if a Russian exile behaves himself decently well, he may in Siberia be more comfortable than in many, and as comfortable as in most of the prisons of the world.' After the year he spent visiting Siberian prisons, Kennan could not agree with Landsell, and revealed the inhumanity of the exile system, the convict mines and the terrible conditions in the overcrowded prisons.

The first exiles

The earliest mention of exile in Russian legal documents was in 1648. In the 17th century exile was used as a way of banishing criminals who had already been punished. In Kennan's words: 'The Russian criminal code of that age was almost incredibly cruel and barbarous. Men were impaled on sharp stakes, hanged and beheaded by the hundred for crimes that would not now be regarded as criminal in any civilized country in the world, while lesser offenders were flogged with the knut (a whip of leather and metal thongs, which could break a man's back with a single blow) and bastinado (cane), branded with hot irons, mutilated by amputation of one or more of their limbs, deprived of their tongues, and suspended in the air by hooks passed under two of their ribs until they died a lingering and miserable death.' Those who survived these ordeals were too mutilated to be of any use so they were then driven out of their villages to the lands beyond the Urals.

The Siberian Boundary Post (circa 1880) In this melancholy scene, friends and relatives bid exiled prisoners farewell beside the brick pillar that marked the western border of Siberia on the Great Post Road.

Exile as a punishment: the convict mines

With the discovery of valuable minerals in Siberia and in light of the shortage of labourers, the government began to use criminals to work the mines. Exile was thus developed into a form of punishment and extended to cover a range of crimes including desertion, assault with intent to kill and vagrancy (when the vagrant was of no use to the army or the community). According to Kennan, exile was also a punishment for offences that now seem nothing short of ridiculous: fortune-telling, prize-fighting, snuff-taking (the snuff-taker was not only banished to Siberia but also had the septum between his nostrils torn out) and driving with reins. Traditionally Russian drivers rode their horses or ran beside them: reins were regarded as too Western, too European.

Abolition of the death penalty

In the 18th century the demand for mine labour grew, and the list of crimes punishable by exile was extended to include drunkenness and wife-beating, the cutting down of trees by serfs, begging with a pretence to being in distress, and setting fire to property accidentally. In 1753 the death penalty was abolished (for all crimes except an attempt on the life of the Tsar) and replaced by exile with hard labour. No attention was given to the treatment of exiles en route, who were simply herded like animals over the Urals, many dying on the way. The system was chaotically corrupt and disorganized, with hardened murderers being set free in Siberia while people convicted of relatively insignificant offences perished down the mines.

Reorganization in the 19th century

In the 19th century the system became more organized but no less corrupt. In 1817 a series of *étapes* (exile stations) was built along the way to provide overnight shelter for the marching parties. They were nothing more than crude log cabins with wooden sleeping platforms. Forwarding prisons were established at Tyumen and Tomsk from where prisoners were sent to their final place of exile. From Tyumen convicts travelled by barge in specially designed cages to Tomsk. From there some would be directed on to Krasnoyarsk or to Irkutsk, a 1670km (1040-mile), three-month march away. Prisoners were sent on to smaller prisons, penal colonies and mines. The most infamous mines were: on the island of Sakhalin, off the east coast, where convicts dug for coal; the gold mines of Kara; and the silver mines of Nerchinsk.

Records were started in 1823 and between this date and 1887, when Kennan consulted the books in Tomsk, 772,979 prisoners had passed through on their way to Siberia. They comprised *katorzhniki* (hard labour convicts), distinguishable by their half-shaved heads; *poselentsi* (penal colonists); *silni* (persons simply banished and allowed to return to European Russia after serving their sentence); and *dobrovolni* (women and children voluntarily accompanying their

(Opposite) Russian Orthodox priests gathering outside St Basil's Cathedral, in Red Square, Moscow.